The Diabolical Game to Win Man's Soul

American University Studies

Series IV
English Language and Literature
Vol. 70

PETER LANG
New York • Bern • Frankfurt am Main • Paris

Dorothy R. Castle

The Diabolical Game to Win Man's Soul

A Rhetorical and Structural Approach to *Mankind*

PETER LANG
New York • Bern • Frankfurt am Main • Paris

Library of Congress Cataloging-in-Publication Data

Castle, Dorothy R. (Dorothy Renshaw)
    The diabolical game to win man's soul : a rhetorical and structural approach to Mankind / Dorothy R. Castle.
        p. cm. — (American university studies. Series IV, English language and literature ; vol. 70)
    Includes bibliographical references.
    1. Mankind (Morality play) 2. Mankind (Fictitious character) 3. Moralities, English—History and criticism. 4. Good and evil in literature. 5. Games in literature. 6. Devil in literature. 7. Soul in literature. I. Title. II. Series.
PR1261.M33C37   1990   89-13662
ISBN 0-8204-1237-6   CIP
ISSN 0741-0700

CIP-Titelaufnahme der Deutschen Bibliothek

Castle, Dorothy R.:
The diabolical game to win man's soul : a rhetorical and structural approach to mankind / Dorothy R. Castle. — New York; Bern; Frankfurt am Main; Paris: Lang, 1990.
   (American University Studies: Ser. 4, English Language and Literature; Vol. 70)
   ISBN 0-8204-1237-6

NE: American University Studies / 04

© Peter Lang Publishing, Inc., New York 1990

All rights reserved.
Reprint or reproduction, even partially, in all forms such as microfilm, xerography, microfiche, microcard, offset strictly prohibited.

Printed by Weihert-Druck GmbH, Darmstadt, West Germany

ACKNOWLEDGMENTS

    I am indebted to many people for the successful completion of this book. My thanks are due to Dr. Turner S. Kobler, whose insightful comments and patient guidance helped me to blend contemporary literary theory with medieval drama; to Dr. Suzanne S. Webb, who introduced me to the possibilities of medieval drama as a fruitful area for research; to Dr. Florence T. Winston, who encouraged me in my efforts with rhetorical analysis; to Dr. Dean Bishop, whose advice and support have been most helpful to me throughout this project; and, especially, to Dr. Lavon B. Fulwiler, who inspired and nurtured my love of medieval literature.

    Others to whom I owe a debt of gratitude are Father Timothy Gollob of Holy Cross Church for his translation of the medieval Latin in the play; Mrs. Carol Toberny for her diligence and patience in deciphering my handwriting and in typing the many drafts of the manuscript; Mrs. Laurie Hammett for typing the final version; Mr. John Leonard for his insight, suggestions, and thoroughness in preparing the camera-ready manuscript and for his brilliant creation of a computer typeface to reproduce the runic character thorn (þ); my dear friends Dr. Cleta Jones, Mrs. Judy Harper, and

Mrs. Pam Luce for their many kind words and prayerful support; Mrs. Alice O'Neal, Mrs. Joan O'Donnell, Mrs. Jacqui Stoneman, and Mrs. Kay Farley for their willingness to interrupt their own plans to help me overcome my frustrations and numerous bouts of writer's block; Mrs. Maxine Washington for her prayers and support; and Dr. Jo Church, to whom I extend my special thanks, for her enthusiastic support, continuous encouragement, clear vision, and wise counsel.

I also wish to express my appreciation to my parents, Joe and Louise Renshaw, and to my sister, Wanda Elliott, for their encouragement and unfailing belief in me. To my daughter, Amy, whose eager interest, consistent optimism, and loving support helped smooth the way for this study, I offer my sincere thanks. And, finally, to my husband, John, without whose love, support, and infinite understanding this project would have been impossible, I wish to extend my very special thanks and deep, abiding gratitude.

Special thanks go to The Council of the Early English Text Society for their permission to reprint quotations from the text of *Mankind* as it appears in their edition of *The Macro Plays: The Castle of Perseverance, Wisdom and Mankind* by Mark Eccles, copyright © 1969 by The Early English Text Society.

Additional acknowledgments for permission to reprint selected material are as follows:

Methuen & Co. for *The Semiotics of Theatre and Drama* by Keir Elam, copyright © 1980.

Yale University Press for *Structuralism in Literature* by Robert Scholes, copyright © 1974.

The University of California Press for *Structuralism and Semiotics* by Terence Hawkes, copyright © 1977 by Terence Hawkes.

Definitions of special biblical terms were taken from *Expository Dictionary of Bible Words* by Lawrence O. Richards, copyright © 1985 by Zondervan Corporation. Used by permission.

Excerpt from the definitions of *Structuralism* from *A Handbook to Literature* by Hugh C. Holman, 5th edition. Copyright © 1986 Macmillan Publishing Company, a division of Macmillan Inc. Reprinted with permission of Macmillan Publishing Co.

Cornell University Press for *The Poetics of Prose* by Tzuetan Todorov translated by Richard Howard, copyright © 1977.

Cornell University Press for *The Pursuit of Signs: Semiotics, Literature, Deconstruction* by Jonathan Culler copyright © 1981 and for *Structuralist Poetics: Structuralism, Linguistics, and the Study of Literature* by Jonathan Culler, copyright © 1975.

Excerpts from *Image-Music-Text* by Roland Barthes. Copyright © 1977 by Roland Barthes. Translation copyright © 1977 by Stephen Heath. Reprinted by permission of Hill and Wang, a division of Farrar, Strauss & Giroux, Inc.

TABLE OF CONTENTS

CHAPTER

I.	Introduction	1
II.	A Rhetorical Analysis of *Mankind* – Part I	17
	A Rhetorical Analysis of *Mankind* – Part II	75
III.	A Linguistic Approach to the Structure of *Mankind*	131
IV.	Conclusion	165
WORKS CITED		189
APPENDIXES		
A.	Todorov's Simple and Complex Transformations	197
B.	Diagrams and Charts	201

CHAPTER ONE

Introduction

The medieval English morality play has long been regarded as a stepchild by medieval English dramatic criticism. Hardly pausing to examine the genre, scholars have had problems even defining the morality play. Most scholars tend to agree with E. K. Chambers that all morality plays contain the clash between Good and Evil (50); however, the consensus ends there, with ideas concerning a more exact definition ranging from Hardin Craig's "dramatized allegory" (341) to Robert Potter's "didactic ritual drama" (*English Morality Play* 57). Although unable to agree on what specifically constitutes a morality play, critics, especially the early critics, generally agree on its lack of merit. Alfred Pollard typifies the reaction of these older scholars when he labels the moralities as "dull and didactic" and their authors as "simple minded" (xliii). David Bevington points out that this scholarly disinterest and aversion result from a belief that the morality play is fragmented, with no plot or organizing principle, and, as such, that it is "artistically insignificant" (2). Critical opinion has been slow to change, but scholars are finally beginning to realize the dramatic value of morality plays as entertainment for modern audiences. This recognition does not extend to the literary value of the manuscripts themselves. Few scholars are willing to mention literary art and the English morality play in the same breath. Although recent efforts have been directed toward form and structure as an indicator of worth, the actual language of the plays has been more or less ignored. Focusing techniques of classical rhetorical analysis and of modern structural analysis on the language of a representative play, such as *Mankind*, reveals the literary artistry of the plays from several angles and is useful in dispelling the negative image of both the morality plays and their authors.

Since judgment concerning the artistic merit of a literary work is often a relatively subjective endeavor based on individual taste and standards, a specific definition of the notion of literary art is required for proper evaluation of *Mankind*. Inasmuch as most scholars do not recognize the literary art of the moralities, few definitions are available from which to choose. Lamenting the almost total lack of articles or books which praise the artistry of the Macro Plays, Michael Kelley analyzes the art of these plays using the coherence of the structural components of the plays as the basis for his work (xi–xii). Kelley centers his study on the controlling structural design rather than on the language (124). Potter, however, argues that the art is that of "objectifying universal ideas in the particularity of dramatic action" ("Divine and Human Justice" 129). Potter is reluctant to render any "exaggerated judgment" regarding a concrete description of the art of the late medieval drama (*English Morality Play* 9). Since neither of these ideas concerning verbal artistry is entirely appropriate for a rhetorical and structural approach to *Mankind*, it becomes necessary to look beyond medieval criticism for a workable theory of literary art. The French linguist Roland Barthes offers just such a theory. Barthes says that "art is without noise" in that "art is a system which is pure, no unit ever goes wasted, however long, however loose, however tenuous may be the thread connecting it to one of the levels of the story" (261). Barthes contends that the pure, distinct, and unobtrusive nature of literary art is what separates art from real life in which fuzzy, indistinct, and blurred communications are the norm. According to Barthes, if fuzziness exists in literary art, it exists as a coded element (261n21), which means that the author has included it for some specific purpose relating to the overall meaning of his work.

The fuzzy communications Barthes describes relate to Victor Shklovsky's theory of defamiliarization as the basis of art. Shklovsky believes that once objects, people, feelings, verbal phrases, and other perceptual messages received from the world at large become commonplace and habitual, these messages also become obscure and indistinct. Perception that has become habitual has become automatic to the extent that conscious awareness of the object of perception tends to disappear (Scholes 83–84). Such a situation creates stereotypes and cliches, causing information to be lost during the process of communication and imparting a dulling quality of inattention and insensitivity to life. As Scholes notes, "Art exists to help us recover the sensation of life; it exists to make us feel things, to make the stone *stony*. The end of art is to give a sensation of the object as seen, not as recognized. The technique of art is to make things 'unfamiliar,' " (83–84). According to Shklovsky's theory of art, one must take something that has grown familiar to the point of near invisibility and defamiliarize it enough to catch the attention of the person involved, forcing him to really "see" the thing, to perceive its reality not just to recognize its existence.

Combining Barthes's notion that "art is without noise" with Shklovsky's theory of defamiliarization results in a useful standard by which to evaluate the literary artistry of *Mankind*, if one accepts the idea that a morality play is a process of defamiliarization. Morality plays present religious teaching in an attention-getting form. They inculcate a moral lesson with a strong ecclesiastical influence (Artz 359). People in the Middle Ages were quite familiar with the rituals of the Mass, the doctrines of the Church, and the threat of damnation. People were also concerned with the hereafter in the fifteenth century (Bennett 100). In spite of this concern, the familiarity with the warnings about sin and damnation in the sermons and by the priests would likely have had the effect described by Shklovsky. The people would listen but not necessarily "hear" the warnings, which were so much a part of their daily lives that these admonitions were taken for granted. By presenting the moral lessons and religious teachings in an entertaining form, the morality plays in general and *Mankind* in particular encourage the audience to focus again on the reality of the Devil's temptation of human beings and the consequences of damnation, rather than simply to accept the existence of that situation. How successful the playwright is in delivering his message depends in large measure on his literary artistry. Since judging the perception and reaction of a medieval audience is not possible, one must examine the playwright's use of language, his literary and rhetorical devices, and his skill with plot and structure in an effort to determine how creatively he has presented the familiar theme of the danger of sin to the human soul. Not only must he approach familiar themes creatively, but the playwright must also incorporate all of the verbal and thematic structures of his play into a cohesive whole with no extraneous parts if he is to achieve the literary art that Barthes labels as being "without noise."

Using the theories of Barthes and Shklovsky as a gauge of the level of artistry, a rhetorical analysis of the playwright's use of rhetorical figures of speech and other verbal structures and of how these rhetorical devices relate to the structure and meaning of the play provides new understanding of *Mankind* from the surface level of the language. Employing the same yardstick of artistic and literary merit, a structural analysis exposes the language of the play from another perspective and yields information concerning the structural units of the plot and the relationships among those units. Rhetorical analysis is a familiar process in the interpretation of literary texts and requires little or no explanation; however, structural analysis is not a familiar process and requires a detailed explanation of the techniques involved.

Although critical theories have evolved since the formulation of structuralism, none of these theories appeared to be as readily adaptable to the requirements of a linguistic analysis of the structure of *Mankind* as the theories of some of the modern structuralists. The definition of structuralism is elusive, varying with individual practitioners of its methodology: "At the heart of the idea of structuralism is the idea of a system: a complete self-regulative entity that adapts to new conditions by transforming its features while retaining its systemic structure" (Scholes 10). Structuralism is mainly a "French movement in contemporary literary criticism utilizing the methods of structural linguistics and structural anthropology" (Holman 430). Linguists such as Ferdinand de Saussure seek the system underneath the language, whereas anthropologists, such as Claude Levi-Strauss, seek the formal systems underlying social cultures (Holman 430). With the aid of structuralism all literary units from the sentence on up can be seen in terms of a system: "In particular, we can look at individual works, literary genres, and the whole of literature as related systems, and at literature as a system within the larger system of human culture" (Scholes 10). Structuralism thus takes a synchronic view of language and literature, which makes it a wide-ranging and extremely ambitious method of literary criticism, especially when one realizes that the underlying system that structuralism seeks is actually a universal grammar.

In an effort to shore up the hypothesis of a universal grammar, Tzvetan Todorov refers to George Boas, who argues that the "appearance of the most fundamental grammatical concepts in every language must be regarded as the proof of the unity of certain fundamental psychological processes" (109). Todorov contends that these psychological premises form the basis for a universal grammar in other symbolic actions as well as in ordinary language (109). Todorov views narrative as just such a symbolic activity, believing that a theory of narrative will shed light on the universal grammar (109). Barthes, Levi-Strauss, and Vladimir Propp agree that such a grammar of narrative exists, arguing that all narratives regardless of their dissimilarity in content and style share "a common structure which is open to analysis, no matter how much patience its formulation requires" (Barthes 253). For the formulation of this theory of narrative structure, Todorov borrows "categories from the rich, conceptual apparatus of linguistic studies," but he avoids following the current language theories too closely (109).

Structuralism, therefore, is similar to the older movement called the New Criticism in that both methods of literary criticism avoid historical and biographical approaches and focus on the text itself. Structuralism differs from the New Criticism in seeking the universal grammar beneath the text, not an interpretation of the meaning. Structuralism aims at a scientific description of the text and the relationships existing among the parts of the text (Todorov 249). As a result of this apparent lack of concern with meaning, the structuralist method has received much negative criticism in the past (Scholes 11); however, some scholars believe that elevating form over content bodes well for increasing our knowledge of how language functions. Jonathan Culler believes that the proliferation of varying interpretations of the same literary works does not assist us in understanding of individual works. In spite of a critical climate that demands interpretation, Culler takes up the position that "while the experience of literature may be an experience of interpreting works, in fact, the interpretation of individual works is only tangentially related to the understanding of literature" (*Pursuit of Signs* 5). Culler argues that the study of literature means "to advance one's understanding of the conventions and operations of an institution, a mode of discourse," not to add yet another interpretation of a Shakespearean play to the large store of existing interpretations (*Pursuit of Signs* 5). In lieu of the interpretation advocated by the New Criticism, Culler suggests studying the relationship between fiction and reality, using a structuralist approach to the operations that define the movement between life and art (*Pursuit of Signs* 6). Poetic diction reflects the author's perceptions about the realities of life. Culler contends that "poetic diction which makes birds 'fish of air' is not an isolated phenomenon; it derives from the general concept of a reversible universe in which one thing is the mirror image of another" (*Structuralist Poetics* 103). He believes that the time has come to focus critical attention on the operations of language and how language evokes meaning and reality. Culler's suggestion that a structural analysis of how art reflects reality would be a worthwhile endeavor might prove useful in the analysis of *Mankind*, whose language exhibits at times this concept of the "reversible universe."

A third group of scholars, represented by Robert Scholes, argues that meaning does not have to be neglected in a structural analysis of a literary work. Scholes believes that interpretation and structuralism can both be used to approach the same text and can yield significations that are complementary to each other rather than opposed to one another (9). Although Culler makes a strong case for the scientific study of language operations exclusive of interpretational overtones, Scholes's position that structuralism and interpretation can profitably be combined appears to be a better solution for the particular critical climate that exists at the moment.

Structuralism has thus far confined its methodology to prose narratives; however, as Barthes points out, "narratives of the world are numberless," and can be found in an endless variety of genres, drama among them (251). Narrative is the story or the plot of the work in question. The techniques employed by structuralists, such as Barthes, Levi-Strauss, and Todorov, in their study of the grammar of narrative can therefore be adapted for use with the drama. These scholars believe that the narrative shares the same characteristics as the sentence and that a "narrative is a long sentence, just as every constative sentence is in a way the rough outline of a short narrative" (Barthes 256). The action of the plot of a drama can be analyzed in similar terms.

Another important structuralist, A. J. Greimas, believes that binary opposition is "the basic human conceptual mode" (Hawkes 90). As a further indication that binary opposition is a fundamental aspect of human thought processes, Claude Levi-Strauss discovered, while analyzing myths from Australia, that a major structural principal of myth is classification by pairs of opposites (*Totemism* 88). The natural species around which the various mythic tales are built require at least one common characteristic that will allow the comparison. According to Levi-Strauss, a binary opposition is "the simplest possible example of a system" (*The Savage Mind* 161). The most explicit example of this principle of binary opposition and its systemic application occurs in China "in the opposition of the two principles of Yang and Yin, as male and female, day and night, summer and winter, the union of which results in an organized totality (*tao*) such as the conjugal pair, the day, or the year" (*Totemism* 89). As the mind expands toward the general and the abstract representation of the real world, it applies a scheme whereby "reality undergoes a series of progressive purifications, whose final term will be provided, as intended, in the form of a simple binary opposition (high and low, right and left, peace and war, etc.)" (*The Savage Mind* 217).

This "basic conceptual mode" appears in the imaginative literature of a culture. The binary opposition employs two actants (functions of character) whose relationship is either oppositional or correlational (Hawkes 90). On the surface level of the narrative, this binary pair's relationship creates the "fundamental actions of disjunction and conjunction, separation and union, struggle and reconciliation, etc." (Hawkes 90). Greimas says that the movement from one opposition to the other involves the transferring of some entity, such as a quality or an object, on the surface structure from one actant to another actant. This movement is the essence of the action in narrative and in drama as well. Binary oppositions can therefore express the underlying thematic contrasts of a literary text. This structural principle is useful in a structural approach to medieval drama that seeks to reveal information concerning both the meaning and the composition. Since one of the few things that medieval scholars agree on concerning the morality plays is that these plays contain the conflict between Good and Evil, an analysis based on binary opposition is particularly relevant.

Another important structuralist, Tzvetan Todorov, offers theories concerning language and literature that are compatible with the theory of binary oppositions and that are equally useful in a structural analysis of medieval morality plays. Todorov's theory applies the same grammatical categories to the structure of literature that are used to describe the structure of language. Todorov suggests that "it is literature which encompasses and explains language," and that it is no longer possible to ignore literature as "a theory of language... if we are to understand literary functioning with the help of linguistic categories" (190). Todorov argues that one can better understand narrative if one looks at the character as a subject/object (noun) and at the action as a predicate (verb). Furthermore, one can understand noun and verb better by looking at the function of these parts of speech in a narrative (119). Todorov thus seeks scientifically to describe a literary text and to establish the relationships among the various elements of that text (249).

An essential aspect of Todorov's theory of poetics is his notion of narrative transformation. Todorov asserts that the value of transformation lies in helping one to understand the essence of narrative, which he defines as "the tension of two formal categories, difference and resemblance" (233). The exclusive presence of either of these elements yields a type of discourse other than narrative. Todorov points out that "transformation represents precisely a synthesis of differences and resemblance" (233). This theory evolved as Todorov studied the research of Victor Shklovsky on the sequence. Shklovsky knew that intuitively people realized when a sequence was complete, but he had trouble articulating his intuition in concrete terms. To clarify his definition he formulated the following rule: " 'The tale requires not only an action but also a reaction, it requires a lack of coincidence' " (Todorov 232). Shklovsky developed six specific examples from the rule, noting that a complete sequence consists of two elements, as depicted in the following chart:

(1) relation of characters → relation of characters inverted

(2) prediction → realization of prediction

(3) riddle proposed → riddle solved

(4) false accusation → accusation dismissed

(5) distorted presentation → correct presentation
    of facts   of facts

(6) motif → parallel motif

(Todorov 232)

Todorov recognized that each of Shklovsky's examples involves a transformation of some type (232). The idea of narrative transformation is therefore quite similar to the notion that for every action there is a reaction. These two actions form a complete entity called a sequence. Sequences combine to form the text of a story. A sequence can be broken down into propositions, which form the basic component unit of the narrative and which consist of the character-action (noun-verb) unit.

Todorov further defines the narrative transformation as the relationship that exists between two propositions when one predicate is the same on both sides. There are two kinds of transformations: simple transformations and complex transformations. Simple transformations modify or add "a certain operator specifying the predicate," since basic predicates have no operators. These transformations roughly correspond to auxiliation in language in which the main verb is modified by a helping verb which specifies the sense of the verb (Todorov 224). Complex transformations occur when a second predicate is attached to the first and cannot stand alone. A simple transformation includes one subject and one verb, whereas a complex transformation has two predicates and either one or two subjects (Todorov 225). Complex transformations delineate "psychic operations or the relation between an event and its representation" (Todorov 225). (Todorov breaks the categories of simple and complex transformations into types, which are discussed in detail in Appendix A.)

If, as Merle Fiefield argues, "the potential vacillation of the will" is actually the connecting element between the dramatic actions (11), another aspect of Todorov's theory of structuralism can prove useful in the analysis of medieval morality plays: his treatment of the moods of narrative predicates. In his analysis of the stories of the *Decameron*, Todorov distinguishes four moods (two dichotomies of mood) based on their relationship to human will (114). The human will is very important in the dramatic structure of the morality plays. Todorov's categories of the moods of the narrative predicate are thus applicable to these medieval plays. His four categories of moods fall into two dichotomies: moods of will and moods of hypothesis. The dichotomy appearing under the moods of will is that of the obligative and the optative. The obligative, which is always present, "is a coded, nonindividual will which constitutes the law of a society" and is an unstated looming presence in the story (114). The optative concerns actions that the characters themselves desire (114). The dichotomy appearing under the moods of the hypothesis is that of the conditional and the predictive. These two moods indicate two succeeding propositions rather than a single proposition (114). The conditional mood refers to the relationship between two propositions in which the subject of one proposition puts a condition on the action of the other proposition. The subject of both propositions is the same. This mood frequently appears as a test in which a maiden will bestow her love only after a certain task is performed successfully (114–15). The predictive mood also concerns two propositions, "but the subject who predicts need not be the subject of the second proposition (the consequence)" (115).

Another important characteristic of narrative predicate is the category of perspectivism. Perspectivism points out that the viewpoint of an action is crucial. Each agent acts as his own hero; therefore, his perspective of the action will be different from the perspective of other agents involved in the same action. According to Claude Bremond, who developed the theory, the possibility and the obligation to shift viewpoints from the perspective of one agent to that of another is crucial to narrative structure. A hero can be a villain from a different perspective. Events in a sequence can have different structurations depending on which agent's interests the structure is based (Todorov 223).

Structuralists, such as Levi-Strauss, Barthes, and Todorov, tend to view narrative plot structure as a three-part entity. Todorov describes narrative plot structure as follows:

> The minimal complete plot consists of the passage from one equilibrium to another. An 'ideal' narrative begins with a stable situation which is disturbed by some power or force. There results a state of disequilibrium; by the action of a force directed in the opposite direction, the equilibrium is re-established; the second equilibrium is similar to the first, but the two are never identical. (111)

This three-part structure will work as well with drama as with narrative. Although most scholars agree with Ramsay that the basic form of the morality play is a four-part structure divided into innocence, temptation, life-in-sin, and repentance (clvi), the three-part structure depicted by the structuralists seems more appropriate as a general dramatic underpinning than the specific categories offered by Ramsay.

Although structuralism is highly theoretical and abstract, theorists have applied its tenets to narrative plot structure in the hope of learning about the functions of a hypothetical universal grammar. Todorov, Barthes, and Levi-Strauss expect that their ideas will be useful as the foundation of other notions about a method of extracting a grammar of narrative. Since narrative is found in all sorts of genres, including drama (Barthes 251), some of the methods used by these structuralists can be adapted for a less ambitious analysis of *Mankind*, one that seeks to expose the play to new angles of inquiry rather than to search for a universal grammar. Using Levi-Strauss's binary pairs as the deep structural foundation of the play, one can analyze the surface discourse in order to determine how these pairs of oppositional forces manifest themselves. A method of analysis based on Todorov's ideas concerning propositions, sequences, transformations, and moods is useful in revealing how the playwright's language on both the syntactic and semantic levels displays his sophistication and artistry.

Adjusting Todorov's definitions of propositions, sequences, transformations, and moods to fit the needs of an analysis of dramatic plot structure requires that one realize that the basic difference between narrative and drama hinges on dialogue. In drama the plot evolves from the character's dialogue, not from narration. Drama is based on "an *I* addressing a *you here* and *now*" (Elam 139). In the discourse of drama "the speaking subject defines everything (including the you-addressee) in terms of his own place in the dramatic world" (Elam 43). The dramatic dialectic is thus based on the exchange between the "I-speaker" and the "you-listener/addressee," who are the only active participants in the drama. Other participants in the drama "are defined negatively by means of the unmarked third person." The others are excluded from the moment and serve as objects of the discourse (Elam 142–43). On the surface level of the drama the grammatical structure "is manifested through various *actants*." An *actant* "may embody itself in a particular character (termed *acteur*), or it may reside in the function of more than one character in respect of their common role in the story's underlying 'oppositional' structure" (Hawkes 89). Todorov's proposition thus becomes, in drama, a basic unit of character interaction. The character who controls the action of the proposition is the subject, and the predicate is whatever action the subject engages in. A sequence is the combination of propositions involved in the same motif and can be identified as a type of anecdotal scene. Transformations refer to the relationships between the propositions as exhibited by the language of the characters. Moods are the secondary grammatical characteristic that is most useful in the analysis of morality plays, because, in Todorov's definition, moods of narrative predicates relate to human will, an important structural aspect of the plays.

Many scholars agree with MacKenzie, who argues that morality plays were dramatic performances acted by real people during the Middle Ages, and that one should not judge them from the manuscripts (*English Moralities* 264); however, through the language of the text, it is possible to get closer to the medieval concept of reality and to evaluate better the play's artistry than it is possible to do through a modern dramatic interpretation. By employing the standard of literary art gleaned from the theories of Barthes and Shklovsky and subjecting the language of the morality play from the Macro Manuscript, *Mankind*, to a rhetorical analysis of the surface structures as they relate to structure and meaning and to a structural analysis based on the theories of Claude Levi-Strauss and Tzvetan Todorov, one gains insight into the literary abilities of the author, as well as insight into the play and, possibly, the genre itself. These two methods of literary inquiry expose *Mankind* from several different angles and yield evidence that aids in counteracting the charge that all of the moralities are "artistically insignificant" and that the authors are "simple minded."

CHAPTER TWO

A Rhetorical Analysis of *Mankind*

Part One

    Morality plays are allegorical presentations of the struggle between the forces of Good and Evil for the soul of Man and are sometimes thought to be a bit dull. The least popular of these plays and the one that appears to have attracted the most strident criticism is *Mankind*. This play has been called everything from "a very degraded type of morality" (Chambers 62) to "a play of the utmost ignorance and crudity" (Craig 350) with one scholar going so far as to label *Mankind* as a dirty play "written for inn-yard amusement" (Rossiter 107). Of the group of critics who find merit in the play, some occupy themselves with questions concerning the source, the author, the audience, the date, and whether the play was performed at Christmas or at Shrovetide, while others concentrate on various ideas about the theme and the reasons that Titivillus is not a proper devil or that Mischief is an extraneous character or that some other aspect of the play does not quite fit.

Until recently no one focused on the language of the play in an effort to prove *Mankind's* value as literary art. Certainly no scholar in either of these two groups would consider *Mankind* as literary art as defined by Victor Shklovsky and Roland Barthes, which is discussed in Chapter One, or as defined by anyone else, for that matter. Although recent critical efforts attempting to validate the literary artistry of *Mankind* have made inroads in adverse scholarly opinion, no one has been able to totally dispel the negative vehemence of early critics and to completely overcome views such as those of David Zesmer, who argues that the author of *Mankind* did not "accurately gauge his artistic effects" and that the Vices revel in the grotesque humor "almost to the point of obscuring the moral purpose for which these characters were introduced" (283). A rhetorical analysis of *Mankind* reveals that the author did indeed "accurately gauge his artistic effects" and that this negative assessment of the play and its author is unwarranted. The author uses his skill with language to make the familiar tenets of Christianity less familiar and more real to the audience and to combine all of the rhetorical elements of the play to support its theme and structure, thereby qualifying *Mankind* as a work of literary art as defined by Shklovsky and Barthes.

The disregard of *Mankind* as a work of literary art occurs among early scholars as a result of the scatological humor, which offended them, and of the presence of comic scenes in a religious drama. The fact that the play has evoked such strong reactions among its critics should be a clue that perhaps true substance lurks beneath the scurrilous language. Hardin Craig is particularly strong in his objections to the play, labeling it as "badly degenerated" and "lewdly vulgarized for the amusement of rural audiences" (343). Arnold Williams agrees with Craig and believes *Mankind* to be "the least learned, least elaborate, earthiest of all the English moral plays" (15). Smart sees the play as a "sham morality" which places the moral lesson in second place to the entertainment factor ("Some Notes on *Mankind*– Concluded" 117). *Mankind* so offended E. K. Chambers that he said that "the monk Hyngham ought to have been ashamed of claiming ownership" (62). In the light of all this righteous indignation, it is ironic that one of the major voices in favor of *Mankind* as a worthwhile play is not at all offended by the slapstick comedy and the vulgar humor. Sister Phillipa Coogan argues that the comic scenes exemplify the moral lessons set up by the allegory of the serious passages (109). The comedy provides negative examples of the homiletic sections (Coogan 91). Bevington agrees with Coogan's assessment of the illustrative value of the humor for the allegory of Mercy's sermons (17). Paula Neuss also espouses the notion that these slapstick scenes make concrete the abstractions of the sermon portions of the play (42). Michael Kelley joins this group of critics who support the view that the comedy is a vital part of the play and that it serves the purpose of illustration (72). A careful examination of the author's use of rhetorical techniques lends support to the theory of this group of critics who find the humor intrinsic to the structural pattern of the play.

Most critics use the scatological humor to bolster their theories about the rural nature of the audience. *Mankind* is a late fifteenth-century play, the exact date being a point of controversy, with some scholars arguing for 1464–69 (Baker 91), some favoring 1470–71 (Smart, "Some Notes on *Mankind*" 47), and others the year 1469 (Jambeck and Lee 513); however, regardless of the specific date, the period of time was one in which audiences were of an earthy nature, and they appreciated scatology on a level that modern audiences cannot relate to at all. The scholars believing that the audience was a rural one whose proximity to farms and animals made them understand this coarse humor are in a majority. People such as Sister Coogan (95), Potter (*English Moral Play* 55), Rossiter (100), Craig (351), Bevington (15), and other respected scholars who hold widely varying opinions on the value of the play itself still feel that the scatological humor proves that the author aimed his play at a relatively uneducated rural audience. Larry Clopper seems to be the lone voice in the wilderness in his argument in favor of an educated rather than a popular audience. As evidence for an educated audience, Clopper points out the large number of untranslated Latin quotations, which the author uses as "authorities to endpoint the argument of redemption" and which appear at the end of the play when the moral lesson is put forth (350). A rhetorical analysis supports Clopper's contention that the audience was educated; however, such analysis does not disprove the notion that a rural audience was also intended. The playwright creatively uses rhetorical techniques in such a way that multiple levels of meaning would have made the play appealing to both a popular and a sophisticated audience.

The playwright's considerable range of rhetorical skills quickly becomes apparent when one subjects the language of Mark Eccles's definitive manuscript of *Mankind* from his edition of *The Macro Plays* to close scrutiny. Employing the medieval rhetorical framework device, the playwright uses Mercy's speeches to frame the action of the play. Mercy's initial speech (11. 1–44) establishes his ethos[1] and sets up images and motifs that echo throughout the play providing thematic support and structural connection. This opening speech can be classified as a form of diatyposis, a speech in which the speaker recommends certain useful rules and ideas to his audience (Joseph 310). In this speech Mercy counsels the audience on the proper behavior if they wish to receive a heavenly reward. Within the first few lines Mercy elaborates on God's power and the necessity of devoted obedience to Him, thus setting up the theme of God's sovereignty over man, which dominates the action of the play:

A Rhetorical Analysis of *Mankind* – Part I

> The very fownder and begynner of owr fyrst
>   creacyon
> Amonge ws synfull wrechys he oweth to be
>   magnyfyede,
> þat for owr dysobedyenc he hade non indygnacyon
> To sende hys own son to be torn and crucyfyede.
> Owr obsequyouse [obedient] servyce to hym xulde
>   be aplyede [devoted].
>   (ll. 1–5)

The playwright uses the figure of antimetabole, in which words are repeated in converse order to sharpen the sense of the words themselves[2] and to emphasize the meaning of the first two lines of the speech: "When he was lorde of all and made all thynge of nought" (l. 6). The first two lines refer to the "very fownder and begynner of owr fyrst creacyon" and the Christian teaching that as lowly sinners we should glorify such a being. The rhetorical emphasis of line six on the word *all* adds another dimension to our understanding of the power of God who ruled over *all* and who created *all* from nothing. A man must give devoted obedience to such a superior being and yield Him sovereignty over one's life. Mercy directs his words specifically to the audience, thereby pulling them into the play as participants and making them part of the play's reality:

> O souerence [gentlemen], I beseche you your
>   condycyons [habits] to rectyfye.
>   (l. 13)
>
> ...
>
> O ȝe souerens þat sytt and ȝe brothern þat stonde
>   ryght wppe.
>   (l. 29)

Again directly addressing the audience Mercy advises them to do good works and to value heavenly things, rather than the material, transitory things of the earth, two motifs that run throughout the play:

> In goode werkys I awyse yow, souerence, to be
>   perseuerante
> To puryfye your sowlys, þat þei be not corupte;
>   (ll. 25-26)
> ...
> Pryke not your felycytes in thyngys transytorye.
> Behold not þe erth, but lyfte your ey wppe.
>   (ll. 30-31)

The author uses the rhetorical figure commoratio to express the idea of Christ's great sacrifice repeatedly in different words, a subtle means of both explaining one of the reasons that God should be glorified and emphasizing the idea from another angle:

> Yt may be seyde and veryfyde, mankynde was dere
>   bought.
> By þe pytuose deth of Jhesu he hade hys remedye.
> He was purgyde of hys defaute þat wrechydly hade
>   wrought
> By hys gloryus passyon, þat blyssyde lauatory.
>   (ll. 9-12)

The idea that "mankynde was dere brought" is set up as verifiable truth in line nine. The "pytuose deth of Jhesu" as Mankind's "remedye" and Mankind's being "purgyde" of his wretched sin by Jesus's "gloryus passyon" are more specific versions of that idea. The author employs isocolon in the four clauses that comprise lines

11 and 12, with eight syllables each in the first clause of each line and seven in the second, to achieve additional emphasis for these different facets of the same idea through syllabic balance of the four clauses and parallel construction in the last two clauses of each line. The rhetorical virtuosity of these four lines lends strong emphasis to the notion that a high price was paid for Mankind, a motif echoing throughout the play in the form of the words "dere bought," classified as the rhetorical figure orcos, which is an oath. This commoratio amplifies the idea that Mankind was "dere bought" and focuses attention on the phrase itself which simultaneously provides a connecting thread for the entire play and emphasizes this theme.

Two words from this passage are associated with water: "purgyde" (1. 11) and "lauatorye" (1. 12). "Lauatorye" is defined as a "cleansing place" or a "washing well" (Eccles 216). "Lauatorye" serves as an appositive for "hys gloryus passyon." These references to water and the appositive connect this passage (11. 9-12) with the water image symbolic of salvation and baptism near the end of Mercy's opening speech, providing a structural link for the whole speech:

> I mene Owr Sauyour, þat was lykynnyde to a lambe;
> ...
> Wyth þe precyose reuer þat runnyth from hys
>   wombe.
> Ther ys non such foode, be water nor by londe,
> So precyouse, so gloryouse, so nedefull to our
>   entent,
> For yt hath dyssoluyde mankynde from þe bytter
>   bonde
> Of þe mortall enmye, þat vemynousse serpente.
>   (11. 34–40)

The repetition of "so" (anaphora) in line 38 produces a hammering effect to drive home the point that Christ's sacrifice provides Mankind with the opportunity to dissolve the bonds of sin with baptismal waters and to accept eternal life. The notion of sacrifice is suggested by the Savior's comparison to a lamb, a common Biblical simile.

Another metaphor worthy of note refers to Christ as the head and to Mankind as the body of the Church:

> Se how þe hede þe members dayly do magnyfye.
> Who ys þe hede forsoth I xall yow certyfye.
> I mene Our Sauyowr,
>
> (11. 32-34)

Mercy uses this metaphor to remind the audience of their position in the scheme of things and to encourage them to fix their attention and allegiance in the proper place with God as their Sovereign Lord.

Mercy uses a familiar metaphor from the Bible to end his speech and to further encourage the audience to adjust their behavior according to the rules he has recounted for them, if they are to be on the winning side at God's Last Judgment:

> The corn xall be sauyde, þe chaffe xall be brente.
>
> (l. 43)

This proverb sums up graphically what Mercy has been saying in different language in the rest of his speech. The worthy shall be saved because they have yielded sovereignty to God, whereas the worthless, who have failed to do this, shall be burned in hell. Since it forms an important structural and thematic link in the first half of the play, this corn metaphor is a form of homoeosis, which teaches a moral lesson by using an extended metaphor.

The corn metaphor also helps Mercy in establishing his ethos with the audience. According to Aristotle the character of the speaker (ethos) "is the most potent of all the means to persuasion" (9); therefore, Mercy must instill in the audience a trust in his honesty and in his concern for their welfare in order to persuade them to take action on his advice. Aristotle points out that audiences are delighted when a speaker uses a maxim or a proverb that states a general truth that they acknowledge (154). Proverbs also produce a moral effect, creating the sense of strong moral character in the minds of the audience. If the speaker did not himself subscribe to the ethical principles involved, he would not utter the maxim (Aristotle 154). Mercy uses the grain proverb to emphasize the idea that those who deny God end up in hell, a fact no medieval audience would dispute. Mercy uses proverbs throughout the play, thus strengthening his ethos with both the audience and Mankind, during the dramatic action.

Another technique that Mercy employs to enhance his ethos and to establish his role in the action of the play is to align himself with God, making it clear that he is God's representative on earth. Several lines in the opening speech achieve this alignment and illustrate the author's ability with antanaclasis, a figure of repetition in which the same word is used with different significations (Taylor 162):

> I haue be þe very mene [mediator] for yowr
>   restytucyon. (1. 17)
> Mercy ys my name,
>   (1. 18)
> ...
> þe grett mercy of Gode, þat ys of most
>   preemmynence,
>   (1. 21)

> I prey Gode at your most nede þat mercy be yowr defendawnte.
>
> (1. 24)

Mercy denotes both the character in the play, who is God's envoy and His mediator for Mankind's soul, and the quality of mercy which allows forgiveness of sins. During the action of the play itself, Mercy becomes more closely aligned with God both directly and indirectly through Mankind's eyes:

> O Mercy, of all grace and vertu ȝe are þe well,
>
> (1. 221)
>
> ...
>
> ȝe be aproxymatt to Gode and nere of hys consell.
>
> (1. 223)

In addition to the specific connection of being "approxymatt to Gode," Mercy is depicted as being the "well" of virtue and grace. The word "well" connects with the water imagery in lines 34–39 of Mercy's opening speech and subtly links Mercy with Jesus Christ.

Many of the thematic motifs and rhetorical devices exhibited in Mercy's opening speech (11. 1–44) are picked up in his last speech at the end of the play to form a frame around the action. Mercy begins his address to the audience after Mankind's departure at the close of the action with an apostrophe, "Wyrschepyll sofereyns" (1. 903), which connects to the first apostrophe to the audience in Mercy's opening speech, "O souerence," (1. 13). The two apostrophes pull the audience into the drama at critical points, making the advice and the warning therein applicable to the gathered crowd. The apostrophes emphasize the frame apparatus. The idea of Satan as Mankind's enemy and captor in Mercy's opening words connects to a similar idea at the end of the play:

> For yt hath dyssoluyde mankynde from þe bytter
> bonde
> Of þe mortall enmye, þat vemynousse serpente,
> From þe wyche Gode preserue yow all at þe last
> jugement!
>
> (ll. 39–41)
>
> ...
>
> God preserue hym fro all wyckyd captiuite.
>
> (l. 905)

Mercy's address to the audience in the final lines of *Mankind* includes a warning about prizing too highly worldly things: "Thynke and remembyr þe world ys but a wanite" (l. 909). This line reflects an important thematic thread in the play and ties into the same warning in Mercy's initial speech: "Pryke not yowr felycytes in thyngys transytorye, / Behold not þe erth, but lyfte yowr ey wppe" (ll. 30–31). Another bit of valuable advice that Mercy offers in this speech, which forms an undercurrent in the action and is reiterated at the end of the play, concerns personal responsibility for one's behavior and the need to account to God for one's actions:

> For sekyrly þer xall be a streyt examynacyon.
>
> (l. 42)
>
> ...
>
> Now for hys lowe þat for receywyd hys humanite,
> Serge ȝour condicyons wyth dew examinacion.
>
> (ll. 907–08)

Mercy wants the audience to realize that he has their best interests at heart and wants them to have their rewards in heaven. All of his advice is aimed at that goal; therefore, the very last lines of *Mankind* ask God to be merciful to the audience and to give them eternal life:

28   A Diabolical Game to Win Man's Soul

> Therefore God grant ȝow all per suam
>   misericordiam
> þat ȝe may be pleyferys wyth þe angellys abowe
> And hawe to ȝour porcyon vitam eternam.
> Amen!
>   (11. 912–14)

This technique is a form of the rhetorical figure optatio, which is defined as an expressed wish. Mercy's desire for God's mercy for the audience is expressed and echoes the sentiments of the optatio of the initial speech quoted above (11. 40–41) in which Mercy prays that God preserve them from the venomous serpent "at þe last jugement." Such genuine concern for the audience's welfare builds Mercy's ethos and becomes a strong element in the framework device.

Another interesting rhetorical ploy that the author sets up in the first eight lines and carries through the entire speech is the repetition of the sound of the letter *s* and the creation of a framework within this opening speech, itself part of the frame around the action of the play. Although not strictly alliteration, the *s*-sound echoes throughout these initial eight lines, giving a hissing sound in the context of a speech about God as our Creator who sacrificed his Son for us disobedient sinners. This device involves voiceless [s], not specifically the letter *s*, at the beginning, the end, and even in the middle of such words as "son," "creacyon," "ws synful wrechys," "dysobedience," "indignacyon," "crucyfyde," "obsequyouse servyce," and "sett" among others. The recurrence of [s] is relatively consistent within the first eight lines. This sibilant [s] thus sets up a contrast between the Devil, represented by the serpent's hiss, and God, the actual subject of the first eight lines. This very subtle rhetorical game establishes the main opponents in the larger game depicted by the action of the play in which God and the Devil square off for the big prize—Man's soul. After the initial eight lines, this clever rhetorical opposition is extended through the rest of the speech. Eccles divides this speech into four stanzas of eight lines each and one stanza of 12 lines. In the twelve-line stanza the Devil is mentioned as "yowr gostly [spiritual] enemy" (1. 27) and in the last stanza is referred to as "þe mortall enmye, þat vemynousse serpente" (1. 40). In this last stanza, which labels the Devil as a serpent, and in the first stanza which rhetorically pits God against Satan, there are 21 [s] sounds, respectively; moreover, in the fourth and longest stanza (12 lines) there are 23 [s] sounds. This stanza deals with the need to do good works to purify the soul, issues a warning about the attempts spiritual foes will make to corrupt Man's good behavior, and includes a reference to Christ as head of the church and the means of salvation. These are all motifs that appear in the action of the play. The increased background hissing symbolizes Satan's urgent need to overcome these obstacles if he is to win Man's soul. The playwright has cleverly used his rhetorical skill to stimulate the unseen presence of Evil, even in the context of a speech uttered by God's representative which has the overtones of a sermon. This unseen Evil in the frame connects to Titivillus's becoming invisible in order to tempt Mankind with his smooth words in the action of the play. Using the same number of [s] sounds in the first and last stanzas of this speech adds balance and symmetry to the speech in addition to providing a rhetorical frame for Mercy's words of wisdom, which themselves provide a frame for the play. This rhetorical dexterity combines with Mercy's elevated vocabulary and elegant imagery to initiate obliquely the theme of the importance of language, which plays a very important role in the action portion of the play.

Having introduced major themes and motifs in Mercy's opening words and having established Mercy's ethos, the playwright extends his rhetorical expertise to the action of the play, employing numerous figures and techniques in an effort to make the familiar Christian themes appear in a new and different way to catch the audience's attention. Analysis of *Mankind* reveals that the play is built on the metaphor of the game. The typical struggle between Good and Evil that characterizes morality plays is thus depicted in *Mankind* as a game between God and the Devil with Mankind's soul going to the winner. As the ultimate forces of good and evil, God and the Devil do not actively participate in the game but are represented on earth by Mercy and Mischief; however, when things do not go according to plan, the Devil, called Titivillus in this play, cheats and takes a personal hand in the action. The game is played with words. Mercy and Mischief exercise their rhetorical talents in an attempt to persuade Mankind to yield sovereignty over his life to God or to Titivillus. Although some recent scholars have focused on the language of *Mankind* and one even refers to the struggle as a battle of words (Ashley 148), no one has recognized the underlying metaphor as that of the game, although the language of the play indicates that the action is a game. In addition to the language, McAlindon's research has also uncovered precedent in medieval literature and drama that supports the notion of a diabolical game as the basis of the contest between good and evil in *Mankind*.

McAlindon argues that a tradition of sinister comedy is apparent in Middle English drama and literature, such as Towneley *Judgement*, Chester *Descent into Hell* (324), and *Sir Gawain and the Green Knight* (329) and is characterized by a mixture of seriousness and jest. The devils in such literary works are endowed with great energy and activity and enjoy giving pain to their victims so much that work becomes sport. These devils "present Hell to their victims as an unending, varied game; it is a parody, an ironic reminder of just those pleasures which betrayed the immoral in life" (McAlindon 324). Encasing such cruelty in the context of a mocking game makes the consequences of sin all the more terrible and gives these comedic scenes their character (McAlindon 324). Some works build the actual conflict around the grim bargain or game, as is the case in *Sir Gawain* (McAlindon 329). Such comedy in medieval religious literature and in works influenced by religious traditions often emerges "directly out of the contemplation of evil to counterpoint a prevailing tone of high seriousness" (McAlindon 323), and in so doing sharpens the sense of the moral lesson involved. This sinister comedy yields a villain who necessarily exhibits comic traits because he satirizes and chastises mankind and displays a witty, sneering, but intelligent character simultaneously. Such villains tend to be powerful and treacherous, depicting evil's ambiguous nature, and are characterized by irony, mockery, and dissimulation (McAlindon 323). This didactic pattern of mixing high seriousness with grim jest and comedy and involving ironic, mocking villains attracted the sophisticated and intelligent writer in the Middle Ages (McAlindon 332). However, the mingling of the serious message with comedy posed potential problems of fear and confusion in the audience, even though such technique usually enhanced the theme. To avoid such problems medieval writers who were adept at their craft "instinctively resorted to the notion of an abominable game, of mocking and blasphemous parody" when they depicted devils or evil characters who possessed the power to test man's faith and courage or the power to inflict pain and punishment (McAlindon 329). With such a literary tradition to inspire him, the author of *Mankind* could go another step and build the entire struggle between God and the Devil for man's soul on the metaphor of the game.

The actual word "game" does not appear in the action until line 69; however, the game begins as soon as Mercy finishes his opening words and is confronted by Mischief, who has overheard Mercy's eloquent words and realizes the high quality of the opposition. A good rhetorical technique of confutation is to make the argument of the opponent appear to be less than it actually is by laughing at it; therefore, Mischief decides to use mockery and derision against Mercy. Employing hypocrisis, the rhetorical figure used to mock an opponent by exaggerating his speech habits or gestures, Mischief greets Mercy with the exact words of the last line of Mercy's initial address to the audience: "I beseche yow hertyly, leue yowr calcacyon,' / Leue yowr chaffe, leue your corn, leue your dalyacyon" (11. 45–46). Not only does Mischief echo Mercy's "I beseche yow hertyly," but he extends Mercy's corn metaphor, which illustrates a serious subject in Mercy's speech, to a very mundane topic, that of complaint about Mercy's excessive chattering. This type of mockery focuses on language and indirectly supports the theme of the importance of language in the play. The use of anaphora, alliteration, and isocolon in successive clauses mocks the pounding style of a preacher who is trying to get his congregation to take action. This rhetorical technique implies that Mercy has been preaching and sets up the next line, which accuses him outright: "Yowr wytt ys lytyll, yowr hede ys mekyll, ȝe are full of predycacyon [preaching]" (1. 47). In this line hypozeuxis, a grammatical scheme of construction endowing each clause with a separate subject and verb, dominates and achieves special emphasis for each separate clause, increasing the derisive impact of the line. The use of the adjective "lytyll" for "wytt" and "mekyll" ("great") for "hede" is almost a form of chiasmus or antimetabole in that there is a crossover in usage. Normally, one refers to "great wit" and "small head," but Mischief wants to display his own wit here and manages to insult Mercy at the same time by implying that Mercy has an exaggerated opinion of himself. The anaphora of "your" and the parallel construction of the clauses add strength to the insult, contributing to the mounting tension, which is relieved by the accusation that Mercy is "full of predycacyon."

Mischief continues to exaggerate Mercy's speech patterns

(hypocrisis) in an effort to mock him and make his arguments appear invalid and absurd. Mischief appeals to Mercy as an expert to clarify a question for him and then poses the question in a singsong gibberish similar to a schoolyard chant:

> But, ser, I prey þis questyon to claryfye:
> Mysse-masche, dryff-draff;
> Sume was corn and sume was chaffe,
> My dame seyde my name was Raffe;
> Onschett yowr lokke and take an halpenye.
> (11. 48-52)

This nonsensical little verse aims to destroy Mercy's serious attempt to make his ominous words graphic by closing his speech with the grain metaphor. Mischief goes a step further and requests money in line 51, thereby aligning himself with the material elements of society and putting forth a connecting link that ties this episode into the collection passage and the Titivillus confrontation with New Gyse, Nowadays, and Nought in the second scene. Smart points out that the phrase "Onschett yowr lekke" joins to Nowadays's latter speech: "Now opyn yowr sachell wyth Laten wordys, / Ande sey me þis in clerycall manere!" (11. 133-34). Both lines represent similar ideas that Smart traces back to the common Old English phrase "wordhord onleac," which means to begin speaking or talking ("Some Notes on *Mankind*" 57). Such an interpretation emphasizes indirectly the theme of the importance of language and achieves further insult to Mercy by asking him to dig into his rhetorical purse and take out his meager offering ("halfpenye") to answer Mischief's absurd question. Eccles says that the line could refer to unlocking one's door (217nM52); however, Smart's theory makes more sense in light of the strong rhetorical theme of the play. The author achieves Mischief's insult to Mercy, an alignment of Mischief with the material world on the literal level, and support for his rhetorical theme on the figurative level with a single line. This entire speech (11. 45–52) in which Mischief tries to undercut Mercy's ethos by maligning his wit and his ego and by disparaging Mercy's opening address as "just preaching" in the hope of wresting the advantage from Mercy exhibits Mischief's command of rhetoric and his own ability with language, making him a worthy opponent for Mercy, who has aligned himself with God in the opening speech.

Mischief aligns himself with the Devil when he sets up the game:

> I say, ser, I am cumme hedyr to make yow game.
> ȝet bade ȝe me not go out in þe Deullys name
> Ande I wyll abyde.
> (11. 69–71)

Mischief implies that the Devil is his master as God is Mercy's, since Mercy ordered him to go away "in Godys name!" (1. 68), and Mischief refuses to leave unless his own master is invoked. Mischief tells Mercy that he came in order "to make yow game," which implies that without the contrast of Evil represented by Mischief there would have been no game or contest for Mankind's soul, and the further indication is that there would also be no play for the audience. These lines thus finally answer Mercy's question to Mischief in line 53 concerning the reason for Mischief's appearance in the first place. The ellipsis which omits the article *a* in front of "game" achieves a second meaning for that word in addition to the struggle for man's soul and that meaning refers to Mischief's making Mercy his own personal game, which sets up the teasing of Mercy in the dancing episode. These lines also reveal Mischief's attitude as frivolous and gleeful about the "game," which actually concerns the serious subject of damnation. This attitude persists throughout the play, placing Mischief in the league with the villains discussed by McAlindon.

Mischief's notion that he is engaged in a game is picked up by Nowadays a few lines later, when he questions Mercy's demand that Nowadays and his friends stop their dancing and when he refers to Mercy's own method of handling his part of the struggle to win Mankind as "pley": "Do wey, goode Adam? do wey? / Thys ys no parte of þi pley" (11. 83–84). Nought takes up the idea of game in lines 85 to 89, when he says he does not enjoy the dancing and that Mercy can try it, if he will take off his clothes in order to "play." This word "play" is an emendation from the manuscript's "pray" (Eccles 156n88), but "play" fits the context better than "pray" unless Nought intends some vague comparison between dancing in his "religion" of devil worship and the ritual of prayer in Christianity represented by Mercy. If the emendation stands, the word "play" then connotes the idea of game set up by Mischief (1. 69) and referred to by Nowadays (1. 84). The reference occurs again several lines later as Mercy prepares to leave Mankind alone with the three rogues, and Nowadays makes disparaging remarks about Mercy's lack of humor: "Men haue lytyll deynte of yowr pley / Because ȝe make no sporte" (11. 267–68). Nowaday's remarks link with the earlier instances of "pley." The continuous references to the battle with Mercy for Mankind as a game heightens the irony of the position of these evil characters, since nothing is more serious than the salvation of the soul. The Devil's minions are immediately put at a disadvantage in this game, because they are not bright enough to realize that winning a soul is not an easy task. The implication is that these three revelers may not be quite intelligent enough to outwit their very serious opponent. Mischief, a more worthy adversary, was driven away during the early part of the action; therefore, the game is in the hands of New Gyse, Nowadays, and Nought.

This element of doubt adds a bit of dramatic intrigue to the scene, enhancing the overall quality of a play in which the outcome is already known to the audience.

During much of the action of the first scene, Mercy addresses the task of teaching Mankind basic Christian doctrine, such as the facts that Christ died to save Mankind's soul from damnation and that Mankind must be God's obedient servant and work hard. Mankind must avoid idleness and the allure of the material world represented by New Gyse, Nowadays, and Nought. Mercy cannot force Mankind to believe his words; the persuasive power of his rhetoric is the only playing device that Mercy has in this game. Mercy must, however, leave Mankind alone with temptation in order to test his strength against the arguments of the opposition. In this game each side works hard to convince Mankind that its way is the better way; however, Mankind must decide where the truth lies, because neither side can force him against his will. The evil forces are trying to separate Mankind from morality and permit his own will to guide him. If they can achieve that, then they will win the game, since fleshly desires will rule in the absence of morality. Mercy's education of Mankind in the ways of God and in proper behavior is all that protects him once Mercy leaves. Before his departure Mercy warns Mankind against Titivillus, the Devil in this play. Mercy expects Titivillus to cheat, as he points out the tools the Devil will use against Mankind:

> Be ware of Tytivillus, for he lesyth [loses] no wey.
> þat goth invysyvll and wyll not be sen.
> He wyll ronde in yowr ere and cast a nett befor
>   yowr ey.
> He ys worst of þem all; Gode lett hym neuer then!
>   (11. 301–04)

Mercy says Titivillus will try anything to entrap Mankind. Titivillus will become invisible, will whisper into Mankind's ear, and will cast a net over his eyes. The net image works well in the context of a game since the equipment of many real games often includes a net. Coogan says that the net is an indication to the audience that the Devil is invisible to Mankind (75), whereas Ashley argues that the net symbolizes the Devil's lies (140). The net probably represents both ideas at the same time. The last phrase in line 304 seems to be a kind of optatio wishing God to prevent Titivillus's interference. Mercy uses the device of ellipsis in which he deletes the word "appear" or some similar word needed to complete the sense of this line ("Gode lett hym neuer then!"), thereby gaining strong emphasis for his plea and depicting the depth of his fear by allowing the negative "neuer" to control the meaning. These lines foreshadow the appearance of the Devil in the second scene and introduce the notion that an actual intervention on his part is an infraction of the rules. Mercy just wants God to keep things fair in this game. God will not appear and neither should the Devil.

The net image helps connect this episode to the last episode in the second scene when another piece of game equipment, a football, is mentioned. By the end of the second scene Mankind has gone from Mercy's side to the side of Mischief and his cohorts. Mankind encounters Mercy and tries to avoid him. The last two lines in the episode belong to New Gyse, who requests a football from the innkeeper: "What how, ostlere, hostlere! Lende ws a football! / Whoppe [hurrah] whow! Anow, anow, anow, anow [enough]! (11. 732-33). The idea of playing football can be interpreted symbolically to mean that Mankind is the football that passes between Mercy and the Devil's helpers. With Mercy's return at the end of the second scene after Mankind has been won over, New Gyse realizes that Mercy will try to convince Mankind to return to his side and the game will continue. The last line (733) echoes New Gyse's frustration with the whole thing, since he has apparently had enough ("anow") of it himself. The epizeuxis, in which "anow" is repeated with no other word intervening, emphasizes the notion that there has been enough of this game, both the literal and the figurative. Sister Coogan recognizes the reference to the football as part of a game that was played on Shrove Tuesday in England and uses it as evidence that the play is a Shrovetide play (8).

In the first scene Mischief leaves at line 71 and is not seen again until the opening of the second scene. Before his departure Mischief informs Mercy that Mischief has appeared in order to "make yow a game" (1. 69). Apparently the "rules" of this game require the adversaries to take turns trying to persuade Mankind to their way of thinking. Mercy gets the first turn by driving Mischief away with overpowering rhetoric. Now since Mercy has left the stage, Mischief's turn has come; however, Mischief fears Mercy is too strong and too persuasive and the game may already be lost. Mischief leaves New Gyse, Nowadays, and Nought to safeguard the Devil's interest and to undermine Mercy during Mischief's absence. New Gyse, Nowadays, and Nought, however, are ineffectual, and Mankind drives them away with his spade. Now Mischief seems to be left at halftime with the game in a shambles:

> Alas, alasse, þat ever I was wrought!
> Alasse þe whyll, I wers þen nought!
> Sythyn I was here, by hym þat me bought,
> I am wtterly ondon!
> I, Myscheff, was here at þe begynnynge of þe game
> Ande arguyde wyth Mercy, Gode gyff hym schame!
> He hath taught Mankynde, wyll I haue be vane
>   [absent],
> To fyght manly ageyn hys fon.
>   (11. 413–20)

The epizeuxis of "alas" in line 413 and the repetition of the word initially in the next line join with Mischief's laments concerning his own calamity, which is a form of threnos (Joseph 390), to paint a verbal picture of anguish. Mischief points out that he was there "at þe begynnynge of þe game" and that he "arguyde with Mercy." Emphasizing these words, Mischief uses the figure ara (a curse) with the phrase "Gode gyfe hym schame!" The game metaphor gains strength from these words and the use of "arguyde" in this context stresses again the importance of language. Since Mischief loses the argument, he is forced to vacate the field, giving Mercy the first chance at Mankind. The situation resembles throwing the dice to determine who gets to be first, except that words are used instead of dice. The phrase in this speech "to fyght manly" echoes Mercy's words when he told Mankind to "resyst lyke a man" (1. 226). This reiteration of Mercy's teaching forms a connecting link between the two scenes.

The mock beheading episode (11. 432–48) can also be seen as support for the game metaphor. The three villains have been injured in various places by their fight with Mankind and are complaining loudly. Mischief offers to ease Nowaday's head pain by cutting off the head and then restoring it again, a service Mischief gladly will extend to New Gyse and Nought as well. New Gyse, Nowadays, and Nought are not taken in by Mischief's facade of good will as he offers to "cure" their pain. Their vehement denials of the need for such drastic measures are in the mode of slapstick comedy. Mischief knows these rogues well and could have anticipated their reactions, thus making a game out of pressuring them to let him try. The possibility exists that this episode was inspired by *Sir Gawain and the Green Knight*, which includes a beheading motif. The Green Knight is able to restore his severed head, but Gawain knows that his own cannot be restored once it is lost. The Green Knight uses Gawain's fears to taunt and tease him in this grim game to dishonor Arthur's best knight. The situations are similar in that a figure with apparent supernatural powers manipulates the fears of less powerful characters in a malicious and sportive fashion. Smart thinks that this episode is influenced by the folklore prototype of the mumming play ("*Mankind* and the Mumming Plays" 24). Regardless of where the author's inspiration comes from, the episode's humor results from Mischief's making sport of the three villains. This episode can be viewed from one level as one of teasing and mocking; however, on a deeper level, the ties to the supernatural remain as a result of Mischief's relationship with Titivillus, a situation indicating that Mischief's occult powers are probably real.

Using good rhetorical technique, Nowadays distracts Mischief from the idea of chopping off injured body parts by changing the subject back to Mankind:

>   Now towchynge þe mater of Mankynde,
>   Lett ws haue an interleccyon [consultation] sythen
>   ȝe be cum hethere.
>   Yt were goode to have an ende.
>
>   (ll. 448-50)

Mischief's side is losing out to Mercy's superior persuasive powers; therefore, this disreputable group must plan a strategy. Time is running out, and, as Nowadays points out in line 450, it is time to end the game. Apparently the strategy the rogues planned with Mischief was to call in the Devil himself, Titivillus, to foil Mercy and win the game by cheating. Again leaving his cohorts in charge, Mischief leaves and does not return until after Titivillus has worked his subtle evil on Mankind and has departed.

Titivillus's words to the audience during his appearance in the second scene lend weight to the theory that he is involved in a diabolical game with God. When Titivillus enters, his first line begins with a Latin phrase meaning "I am lord of lords": "Ego sum dominacium dominus and my name ys Titivillus" (1. 475). This line puts Titivillus on the same level as God, who is described by Mercy in line six as "lorde of all." Titivillus sends New Gyse, Nowadays, and Nought out to do his bidding and then addresses the audience, telling them his plan to wrest Mankind from Mercy and describing his procedure:

> Euer I go invysybull, yt ys my jett [custom],
> ande befor hys ey þus I wyll hange my nett
> To blench [deceive] hys syght; I hope to haue hys
> fote-mett [take his measure].
> (11. 529-31)

These lines fulfill Mercy's words of warning and provide another structural link between the first two scenes, as well as corroboration of Mercy's words of warning as truth:

> Be ware of Tytivillus for he lesyth no wey,
> þat goth invysybull and wyll not be sen.
> He wyll ronde [whisper] in yowr ere and cast a nett
> before yowr ey.
> (11. 301-03)

This idea of the devil's distortion of Mankind's eyesight with a net is part of literary tradition; however, the image also has similarities to the ancient children's game of Blind Man's Bluff. Mankind is certainly blinded to reality by the Devil's net and must "feel" his way around, relying on the voices of other players as his guide.

Titivillus again reminds the audience of his plan to lure Mankind to his side in this game:

> I trow Mankynde wyll cum ageyn son,
> Or ellys I fere me ewynsonge wyll be don.
> Hys bedys xall be trysyde [snatched] asyde and þat
>   anon.
> ȝe xall a good sport yf ȝe wyll abyde.
>
> (ll. 573-76)

The use of the word "sport" in line 576 indicates the idea of a game at the expense of Mankind. A few lines later Titivillus refers to the proceedings as a game: "A praty [clever] game xall be scheude yow or [before] ȝe go hens" (l. 591). When Titivillus finishes his work on Mankind, he again describes his actions as a game: "Farwell, euerychon! for I have don my game / For I have brought Mankynde to myscheff and to schame" (ll. 605-06). Titivillus points out that the object of his game was to bring Mankind, in this context both literally and symbolically, to mischief (Mischief). The shame of this situation occurs when Mankind finally realizes how he was duped.

After Titivillus's departure and upon hearing about Mankind's "dream" that Mercy has been hanged as a horse thief, Nowadays realizes that Titivillus caused it to happen:

> I sey, New Gyse, Nought, Tytivillus made all þis:
> As sekyn [certain] as Gode ys in hewyn, so yt ys.
>
> (ll. 659-60)

Using a religious simile to enhance the truth of his observation, Nowadays also reveals the essence of what has transpired. God is indeed in His heaven where He should be, allowing Mercy to be His representative in this game on earth; however, Mankind's dream is proof enough that Titivillus has cheated and has come to earth to intervene on behalf of his ineffectual followers in order to prevent losing the game altogether.

In the last scene Mankind confesses that Titivillus has used his net to lead Mankind astray; however, Mercy reminds Mankind that he was forewarned but chose to ignore the warning:

> Mankend, ʒe were obliuyows of my doctrine
> > monytorye [warning instruction].
> I seyd before, Titiuillus wold asay ʒow a bronte [try
> > to attack you].
> Be ware fro hensforth of hys fablys [lies] delusory.
> > (ll. 879-81)

Mercy gently chastises Mankind for ignoring the earlier warning and reminds Mankind to beware of Titivillus's lies "hensforth." This word implies that the game is not over and that another round may be in the offing. Mankind's confession that Titivillus caused Mankind's defection by lies and subterfuge indicates that he will be better prepared to meet the Devil in the next round of this game:

> A, yt swemyth [grieves] my hert to thynk how
> > onwysely I hawe wroght.
> Tytiuillus, þat goth invisibele, hyng hys nett before
> > my eye
> And by hys fantasticall visionys sediciusly sowght,
> To New Gyse, Nowadayis, Nowght causyd me to
> > obey.
> > (ll. 875-78)

Mankind has perhaps become a bit wiser for his experience with Titivillus and will fare better in the next encounter. Before Mercy sends Mankind away at the end of the play, he warns Mankind again about Titivillus: "Be ware of Titivillus wyth his net..." (l. 895). Although somewhat experienced now, Mankind must still be cautioned because this diabolical game will continue until Mankind dies. The victor will be the one in possession of Mankind's soul, the symbolic football, when he dies and the contest can go no further. Mercy makes it clear that Mankind must accept God's mercy and thus yield Him sovereignty while Mankind still lives if he is to enjoy heavenly bliss:

> In þis present lyfe mercy ys plente, tyll deth
> makyth hys dywysion;
> But whan ze be go, vsque ad minimum quadrantem
> [even to the ends of the earth] ȝe shall rekyn
> ȝour ryght [due reward].
> Aske mercy and hawe, whyll þe body wyth þe sowle
> hath hys annexion;
> Yf ye tary tyll your dyscesse, ȝe may hap [chance of
> your desyre to mysse [fail].
> (11. 861–64)

These strong warning speeches at the end of the play are proof that the threat to Mankind's soul will exist until his death. He must be strong and must adhere to Mercy's doctrine. The warning to "Beware of Titivillus" echoes Mercy's initial warning in the first scene and connects to the fruition of his prophetic words in the second scene when Titivillus tells the audience in almost the same words that Mercy used that he plans to become invisible and use his net to delude Mankind. This same idea appears in Mankind's confession in the third scene that Titivillus became invisible and deceived Mankind with his net. Mercy's final warning to "Be ware of Titivillus" effectively ties off a connecting thread that runs through all three scenes of the play, underscoring the notion for both Mankind and the audience that they must "beware," because the Devil will be in this game to the very end in the hope of possessing their souls at the time of death.

The object of this diabolical game is the sovereignty over Mankind's soul. Although most scholars seem to focus on sloth as the major theme in *Mankind*, with Stock arguing for patience (406) and Williams for sin and repentance (16), the dominating theme is sovereignty over the soul of Mankind, which Mercy sets up in his opening speech in the play. This sovereignty theme is then strengthened through imagery, recurring motifs, and other rhetorical techniques throughout the action of the play. When Mercy sets up the sovereignty theme in his opening speech, he argues persuasively that Mankind must yield sovereignty over his life to God and become His obedient servant. God's sovereignty over Mankind is uppermost in Mercy's mind in this speech, which has been discussed in detail in the earlier part of this chapter dealing with the framework device. In that speech Mercy points out that "mankynde was dere bought" (1. 9), a phrase that emphasizes the high price Christ paid to redeem Mankind's soul and that implies the importance of accepting the sacrifice and God's sovereignty. This phrase becomes a recurring motif in the action of the play. Mercy uses this reference to Christ's sacrifice again during a confrontation with New Gyse, Nowadays, and Nought: "Be Jhesu Cryst þat me dere bowte / ȝe betray many men" (ll. 116–17). This particular line juxtaposes the oath (orcos) with a reference to Judas, whose betrayal of one man, Christ, set in motion the means for the crucifixion, which is the meaning of "dere bowte." By accusing the three rogues of betraying many men in the context of the "dere bowte" oath, Mercy subtly links them with the worst betrayer of them all. Several lines later Mercy uses the oath again to remind Mankind gently of his connection to God and to give the weight of God's authority to his words of warning:

All to son, my brother, I fere me, for yow

> He was here ryght now by hym þat bowte me dere,
> Wyth oþer of hys felouse; þei kan moche sorow.
>
> (ll. 254–56)

Mercy employs an indirect reference to the "dere bowte" oath to lend the heavy weight of truth to his words and to encourage Mankind to be attentive to the advice: "Lose not thorow foly þat ys bowte so dere" (l. 282). The line follows two offstage speeches by Nowadays and Nought, which graphically depict the follies to which Mankind can fall victim. Mercy is trying to point up the fact that New Gyse, Nowadays, and Nought are utter fools, the epitome of fools who have lost their spiritual reward. The implication is that Mankind will not be as foolish as the three misfits, but the possibility exists. The idea of folly is thus tied into the heart of the play through the use of the "dere bowte" oath, a reminder of Christ's sacrifice, and the juxtaposition of the line to the two speeches by Nowadays and Nought, men who have foolishly refused to accept the sacrifice of Christ and to yield sovereignty over their souls to God.

The "dere bowte" oath is not limited to Mercy. Mischief and New Gyse use it in the second scene, which creates a structural link between the two scenes. Mischief echoes Mercy's favorite oath during his lament at the opening of the second scene, when Mischief believes that Mercy has won the game: "Sythyn I was here, by hym þat me bought, / I am wtterly ondon" (ll. 416–17). Coming from Mischief's mouth the oath acquires an ironic quality. Although literally Christ died for all mankind, Mischief has made his choice already to serve the Devil; therefore, instead of Christ, the "hym" in Mischief's case refers to the Devil, even though Mischief himself is unaware of the dramatic irony that he is creating. New Gyse uses the oath when he runs into the scene as if someone were chasing him:

> Make space, for cokkys body sakyrde, make space!
> A ha! well ouerron! God gyff hym ewyll grace!
> We were nere Sent Patrykes wey, by hym þat me
>   bought.
>
>   (ll. 612-14)

The use of epanalepsis, the repetition of "make space" at the beginning and end of the line, and of diacope, the separation of the initial and final phrase by an oath (orcos), effectively grabs the audience's attention and emphasizes New Gyse's severe agitation. The oath "for cokkys body sakyrde" is a religious oath meaning "by the Sacrament," just as the vehement supplication to God (deesis) to pour evil on the man chasing New Gyse is also a religious ploy. In the mouth of an evil man like New Gyse the religious connotations reveal that a vestige of belief lingers, thus making New Gyse's following of Titivillus a personal choice rather than a lack of belief in God. The two religious oaths along with the oath "by hym þat me bought" are an effort on New Gyse's part to lend credibility and emphasis to his words. Since New Gyse is also the Devil's man not God's, irony is present in his use of the oath. This reference to Mercy's favorite oath ties into all of the other references linking the parts of the play together and gaining oblique support for the sovereignty theme through the connection to Christ's sacrifice for Mankind's salvation. Eccles's notes to *Mankind* point out that both Herod and Cain use the oath " 'by hym that me dere boght' " in the Towneley plays (218nM116); therefore, the oath may be a literary convention to which the playwright has given a creative twist by using it for emphasis, for dramatic irony, and as a structural link in the play. If the oath is a literary convention familiar to the audience, the playwright has given it a new significance in his play, which will make an audience aware of it and, possibly, truly absorb its meaning.

The playwright uses another image based on a familiar proverb to support the sovereignty theme from a different angle to support the sovereignty theme from a different angle and to achieve additional structural unity. To illustrate the consequences of failure to yield sovereignty over one's soul to God, the playwright employs the corn proverb of John the Baptist (Matt. 3:12; Luke 3:17). Mercy initiates this recurring motif in his opening speech when he ends his words of advice on Christian behavior with the corn proverb:

> þat vemynousse serpente,
> From þe wyche Gode preserue yow all at þe last
>   jugement!
> For sekyrly þer xall be a streyt examynacyon,
> The corn xall be sauyde, þe chaffe xall be brente.
> I besech yow hertyly, haue þis premedytacyon.
>   (11. 40–44)

Mercy metaphorically aligns those who let God guide their lives with the corn and those who refuse God and follow the Devil's ways with the chaff. Mercy warns that there will be a "streyt examynacyon" (1. 42) and that the corn will be separated from the chaff, which will be destroyed. One must obey God and follow His teachings, if one is to be counted as part of the corn at Judgment Day. This idea, exhibited as different facets of this corn-chaff metaphor, weaves in and out of the first scene and is picked up by Titivillus in the second scene, thus providing a unifying strand, as well as thematic support.

Mischief is the first character in the action of the play to incorporate the grain metaphor into his speech, and he uses it in an effort to mock Mercy and to ridicule his language and beliefs:

> But, ser, I prey þis questyon to claryfe:

Mysse-masche, dryff-draff,
Sume was corn and sume was chaffe,
My dame seyde my name was Raffe.

(ll. 48-51)

Mischief continues on in the same mocking vein in his second speech in the first scene:

For a wynter corn-threscher, ser, I haue hyryde,
Ande ȝe sayde þe corn xulde be sauyde and þe chaff
    xulde be feryde,
Ande he prouyth nay, as yt schewth be þis werse:
'Corn seruit bredibus, chaffe horsibus, straw
    fyrybusque.'
Thys ys as moche to say, to yowr leude
    wndyrstondynge,
As þe corn xall serue to [for] brede at þe nexte
    bakynge.
'Chaff horsybus et reliqua,
The chaff to horse xall be goode provente,
When a man ys forcolde þe straw may be brent,
And so forth, et cetera.

(ll. 54-63)

Davenport believes that these speeches symbolize Mischief's challenge to both Mercy and the familiar corn metaphor of John the Baptist. Davenport argues that Mischief's rendition of the metaphor is chiefly to correct Mercy's inaccuracy and to reveal the practical reality of threshing corn. To Davenport Mischief is quite literal and Mercy is metaphorical (38). In a certain sense this theory has some merit; however, in the context of the game metaphor on which the play is constructed, Mischief is being a bit symbolic as well. When Mercy asks Mischief why he came there and tells him he was "not dysyrde" (1. 53), Mischief's answer could be construed in two ways: "For a wynter corn threscher, ser, I have hyryde" (1. 54). Either Mischief has hired a winter corn-thresher, or he himself has hired on as a corn-thresher. Understanding Mercy's metaphorical comparison of the corn to those who give God sovereignty and obey His doctrine, Mischief has come into the scene to provide the opposition. He plans to do a little "corn-threshing" of his own and to persuade some of those people who are part of the corn to become part of the chaff. Possibly, if Mischief himself is not the corn-thresher and he has "hyryde" one, Mischief could already be formulating plans to have Titivillus step into the game to cut down the corn and put it in their barn instead of God's. The mocking tone of the rest of the speech indicates that Mischief is trying to defuse Mercy's persuasive influence. The use of the "English-Latin" vocabulary in the verse is an intolerable vice of language (Joseph 300), and a rhetorical blunder that Mercy would never commit; however, Mischief speaks his coined foreign language in good rhetorical style with the figure prozeugma, which allows the first stated verb to serve the other two clauses without restatement (Joseph 296), thereby gaining emphasis for his furtive mockery of the clergy, who quotes Latin verses, his direct ridicule of Mercy's superior presence, and his alignment of corn with bread, chaff with horses, and straw with fire. This particular alignment has the practical and literal overtones Davenport spoke of and is another side to Mischief's overall attempt to discredit Mercy. Mischief's use of the corn metaphor serves not only as a connecting element in the play's structure, but also as an indirect support of the sovereignty theme because Mischief's attempts to undermine Mercy, who represents God's sovereignty, are subtle efforts to reveal such sovereignty as a poor choice. If this play is successful, then Mischief will have laid the groundwork for the people to follow the Devil as their sovereign lord and for the victory of his side in this game.

Another instance of roundabout support of the sovereignty theme through the use of a maxim that connects to the grain metaphor is found in Mercy's speech:

> Then xall I, Mercy, begyn sore to wepe;
> Noþer comfort nor cownsell þer xall non be hade;
> But such as þei haue sown, such xall þei repe.
> þei be wanton, but þen xall þei be sade.
>
> (ll. 178-81)

Another aspect of the corn metaphor appears in the proverb that says that one reaps what he sows. If one has made God his Sovereign Lord, then he will behave in a fashion that will allow him to reap rewards in heaven. If one has not allowed God to be his Lord, then that person's behavior will yield punishment in hell. This facet of the corn metaphor supports the sovereignty theme from another angle and underscores the themes of good deeds and honest work along with the rhetorical theme, since one sows words as well as deeds. The rhetorical device of anaphora, which allows the repetition of "such" at the beginning of each of the two clauses in line 180 in conjunction with the isocolon, which balances the syllables, and the parallel construction focuses attention on these lines. The chiasmus of "þei have" and "xall þei" within the parallel construction of the two clauses emphasizes the verbs "sowyn" and "repe," which occupy the important end position of each clause. The same situation prevails in the next line, except that the effect is created by antithesis of the words "wanton" and "sade" rather than chiasmus of subject and auxiliary verb in each clause; consequently, the greatest stress is placed rhetorically on the verbs, implying from yet another direction that one's actions are all important, especially if a place among the corn is desired. Mercy extends this idea further in the last lines of his speech and applies it to the situation at hand:

> The goode new gyse nowadays I wyll not dysalow.
> I dyscomende þe vycyouse gyse; I prey haue me
>   excusyde,
> I nede not speke of yt, yowr reson wyll tell it yow.
> Take þhat ys to be takyn and leue þat ys to be
>   refusyde.
>   (11. 182-85)

In this speech Mercy seems to be applying a version of the corn metaphor to the situation existing in the world at that moment. The virtuous new fashion ("goode new gyse") Mercy will not dispraise, but he finds fault with the vicious manner of living ("vycyouse gyse"). Perhaps Mercy means that new ways are not bad because they are new; they are bad only if they violate the Christian way of living and threaten God's sovereignty. One must choose proper behavior from among fashionable trends and must avoid the rest. This advice is another aspect of the "reap what you sow" idea with its subtle connection to the corn metaphor. Mercy flatters the audience by begging forgiveness that he would dare to speak of something that they were reasonable enough to see for themselves. Saying that he "nede not speke of yt," when he has already spoken of it specifically in the previous two lines and generally in the whole speech is a form of the rhetorical device occupatio in which one draws pointed attention to a matter by appearing to pass over it. By ending his speech with a reference to a different facet of the corn proverb, Mercy provides a link between this speech, the opening speech, and the other instances of the grain metaphor appearing in the action of the play. In addition to structural support, Mercy achieves major emphasis for the themes of sovereignty and free will. The corn chaff metaphor originally symbolizes God's choice of those morally good and deserving of heaven and His rejection of those immoral and unworthy. Couching the same idea in ordinary language puts Mankind in the role of choosing the way he plans to live. If he takes the good aspects of the new fashion for living into his own lifestyle, as the metaphor suggests, and refuses to engage in the evil elements portrayed by New Gyse, Nowadays, and Nought, then Mankind (and the audience) can be assured of being the "corn" and not the "chaff."

In the episode in which Nowadays and his friends harass Mankind as he plants his corn, Nowadays makes a reference to corn that is worthy of note in relation to the grain proverb. Nowadays's words refer to literal corn; however, symbolically, the corn can refer to Mankind's good works and to the fruit of honest toil in this context:

> Xall all þis corn grow here
> þat ȝe xall have þe nexte ȝer?
> Yf yt be so, corn hade nede be dere,
> Ellys Ve xall haue a pore lyffe.
> (11. 352–55)

Nowadays does not think much of Mankind's meager corn crop, believing it to be insufficient to support Mankind unless corn brings a high price. The corn symbolizes Mankind's good works and honest toil on earth according to the doctrines of his Sovereign Lord, and, as such, it is priceless, hence the irony of Nowadays's remarks. These lines support the sovereignty theme from the angle of actions: obedient servants of God engage in good works and honest toil as God directs and shall be rewarded in heaven for their obedience.

Further support for the sovereignty theme comes through a negative reference to corn. Nought composes a scatological little rhyme about Mankind's ability to water and fertilize the corn crop all by himself, producing his own "rain" and "fertilizer":

> Here xall be goode corn, he may not mysse yt;
> Yf he wyll haue reyn he may ouerpysse yt
> Ande yf he wyll haue compasse he may
>   ouerblysse yt
> A lytyll wyth hys ars lyke.
>   (ll. 372–75)

These lewd allusions and the unpleasant language of the jingle are technically the rhetorical device known as aischrologia. The implication of these lines is that Mankind does not need Nature to help with his crop, since he can provide everything necessary himself. Extending the symbolism to include God, who controls Nature, one can see that Nought is subtly planting seeds of his own in Mankind's mind. Mankind does not need God or Nature, if he can handle things himself. These seeds of pride take root when Mankind routs New Gyse, Nowadays, and Nought with his spade and, for a time, exults in his own personal victory over the villains. The playwright uses the filthy allusions and the foul language of the rhyme to convey the foulness of the idea of trying to get along in life without God.

Titivillus exposes another facet to the corn metaphor that enhances the sovereignty theme from the negative side. As part of his scheme against Mankind, Titivillus mixes weeds with the corn for planting:

> I xall menge [mix] hys corne wyth drawke and
>   wyth durnell;

Yt xall not be lyke [fit] to sow nor to sell.
Yondyr he commyth; I prey of cownsell [secrecy].
He xall wene [think] grace were wane [lacking].
(11. 537–40)

By mixing the two common weeds in with the seed corn, Titivillus contaminates the corn so that it becomes useless to Mankind. On a symbolic level Titivillus is planning to mix New Gyse, Nowadays, and Nought, who are definite weeds, with Mankind, who is the corn of the corn-chaff metaphor. By contaminating Mankind with the three rogues, Titivillus hopes to pollute Mankind's moral character, making him useless to Mercy and thereby winning the game of sovereignty over Mankind's soul.

In an effort to add depth and dimension to the theme of sovereignty, the author employs other images that reflect the struggle between God and the Devil for supremacy over Mankind on different levels. For example, the contest between husband and wife for control of the marriage appears in the relationship between Nowadays and his wife Rachell:

Also, I haue a wyf, her name ys Rachell;
Betuyx her and me was a gret batell;
Ande fayn of yow I wolde here tell
Who was þe most master.
(1. 135–38)

Nought quickly responds to this remark: "Thy wyf Rachell, I dare by twenti lyse" (1. 139). Nowadays's instant anger indicates that Nought's assessment of the domestic situation is right on target: "Who spake to þe, foll? þou art not wyse!" (1. 140). This episode dealing with domestic sovereignty brings to mind the same theme in *The Canterbury Tales*. The raging battle between Rachell and Nowadays could easily be that between the Wife of Bath and

Jankin, particularly in light of Nought's remarks which come in response to Nowadays's command to him, "Osculare fundamentum!" ["kiss my bottom"] and are reminiscent of a similar situation in *The Miller's Tale*:

> Lo, master, lo here ys a pardon bely-mett.
> Yt ys grawntyde of Pope Pokett,
> Yf ȝe wyll putt yowr nose in hys wyffs sokett,
> ȝe zall have forty days of pardon.
> (ll. 143–46)

Although sovereignty is mentioned specifically in the *Wife of Bath's Prologue* along with the word *maistrie* (*mastery*) in the context of the state of marriage, sovereignty is not mentioned in *The Miller's Tale*. *The Miller's Tale* does, however, deal with a young wife, Alison, who collaborates with her lover to fool her old husband into believing a second flood is coming and who puts her bottom out the window for an admirer, Absalon, to kiss. Such a woman is definitely in control of the marriage. Line 145 reflects the incident between Alison and Absalon, and the "forty days of pardon" of line 146 in *Mankind* could be construed in this context as a reference to the flood. Absalon is an effeminate parish clerk and, therefore, for the purpose of satire, his lowly connection with the Church could be elevated to that of "Pope." Although Jambeck and Lee believe that they have traced historically a real John Pokett who was prior at Barnwell Abbey (512), it is still possible that the author might have seen a parallel in an intended and oblique reference to Absalon, given the context of the sovereignty theme. And, of course, there is a noteworthy connection to medieval drama in *The Miller's Tale* in the form of Absalon's performance as Herod. Stretching the possible allusion still further, Nowadays's speech a few lines later calls for sudden blindness to be sent to Mercy, which is the fate of the old merchant in *The Merchant's Tale* in which a young wife also cuckolds her husband and is master of the marriage:

> Cum wynde, cum reyn,
> Thou I cumme never ageyn!
> þe Deull put out both yowr eyn!
> Felouse go we hens tyght.
> (ll. 154-57)

After Mercy has told them to leave and Nowadays has spoken his rhyme, Nought makes a reference that lends credibility to the notion that *The Canterbury Tales* may have influenced the previous lines dealing with the sovereignty theme:

> Go we hens, a deull wey!
> Here ys þe dore, her ys þe way.
> Farwell, jentyll Jaffrey,
> I prey Gode gyf yow good nyght!
> (ll. 158-61)

According to Eccles, some scholars have traced these lines to proverbs, a quite plausible theory; however, in light of the previous references to Pope Pokett and similar lines that seem to reflect the influence of *The Canterbury Tales*, the mention of "jentyll Jaffrey" could be deliberate. By putting this particular proverb in the mouth of Nought, the playwright closes off the allusion to Chaucer and *The Canterbury Tales* in a skillfully rhetorical way that Chaucer himself might have been pleased with.

Of course, there is no conclusive way to prove Chaucerian influence in these lines, although circumstantial evidence helps support the possibility. Chaucer was widely read and imitated in the fifteenth century by such literary figures as John Lydgate, Thomas Hocclew, John Skelton, and William Dunbar (Zesmer 260).

Judging by the number of surviving manuscripts, *The Canterbury Tales* were read by many people far and wide but were not as highly regarded critically as *Troilus* and other works by Chaucer (Pearsall 202). Chaucer was certainly ribald and bawdy in his humor at times. Underlying ribaldry and scatological humor is Chaucer's concern with moral and theological questions and a genuine wish to improve humanity (Brewer 249). Since Chaucer was a relatively popular author with fifteenth-century readers and his admirable moral purpose supported his bawdy humor, it is not surprising that the author of *Mankind*, who was probably a cleric of some sort, might be drawn to read Chaucer and be influenced by him, especially in terms of using a sovereignty theme in a morality play.

The author uses another instance of the domestic sovereignty idea later in the play. Nought contradicts Nowadays's estimation that Mankind's crop is too small to support him by saying that his crop is such that Mankind "xall never spende yt alonne; / I xall assay to gett yow a wyffe" (11. 358–58). This reference to a wife who spends her husband's money obliquely underscores the theme of sovereignty, since the one who controls the money controls the marriage. These lines connect to the earlier mention of the domestic struggle between Nowadays and Rachell and provide another unifying thread for the play.

The dichotomy between the body and the soul, which is introduced in Mankind's initial speech (11. 186–216), is another image incorporated by the playwright into the action to support the sovereignty theme. Mankind mentions the body-soul contest in the third stanza of his first speech in the play:

> My name ys Mankynde. I haue my composycyon
> Of a body and of a soull, of condycyon contrarye.
> Betwyx þem tweyn ys a grett dyvisyon,

> He þat xulde be subjecte, now he hath þe victory.
> (11. 194–97)

Mankind thus introduces a different angle of the sovereignty theme, that of the body over the soul. The isocolon of the two clauses and the antithesis of the one who ought to be "subjecte" and the one who now has the "victory" emphasize the notion of "condycyon contrarye" in line 195, which is the major theme of this speech and a recurring motif in the play. Mankind laments the body's control over the soul and mentions domestic sovereignty between husband and wife:

> Thys ys to me a lamentable story
> To se my flesch of my soull to haue gouernance.
> Wher þe goodewyff ys master, þe godeman may
>   be sory.
> I may both syth and sobbe, þis ys a pytuose
>   remembrance.
> (11. 198–201)

The juxtaposition of the first two lines dealing with the body's rule of the soul with the second two lines dealing with the wife's rule of the husband implicitly designates the husband-wife relationship as a metaphor for the body-soul conflict. This metaphorical comparison joins the two images which present different facets of the sovereignty theme and recalls the earlier image of domestic sovereignty illustrated by the relationship between Nowadays and Rachell (11. 135–46). The link between the Nowadays-Rachell episode and this "goodewyff-goodeman" image forms a structural connection that aids in the unification of the parts of the play. Mankind points out that man's desires are voluntary:

> Euery man for hys degre I trust xall be partycypatt,
> Yf we wyll mortyfye owr carnall condycyon
> Ande owr voluntarye dysyres, þat euer be
> pervercyonatt,
> To renunce þem and yelde ws wnder Godys
> provycyon.
>
> (ll. 190–93)

The emphasis is on the necessity of bringing the "voluntarye dysyres" of the body under control and yielding to God's "provycyon" ("providence"). God, who is a part of Man's soul by virtue of the creation, must be in control, not Mankind. Mankind then uses apostrophe to address the soul and to emphasize the distress that he feels at the unfairness of such a wonderful entity being shackled by the filth of Man's flesh:

> O thou my soull, so sotyll in thy substance,
> Alasse, what was þi fortune and þi chaunce
> To be assocyat wyth my flesch, þat stynkyng
> dungehyll?
>
> (ll. 202–04)

The alliteration of voiceless [s] in the first line emphasizes the important words in the line, the "sotyll" (delicate) "substance" of the "soull." The rhetorical question is a form of epiplexis in which one questions in order to rebuke; however, the insult is directed at the body not the soul. The appositive for "flesche," "þat stynkyng dungehyll," contrasts vividly with "sotyll substance," pointing up the dichotomy of the body and soul and emphasizing the vast chasm between these contrary entities. The appositive also links the flesh or the body with a dunghill, which is important in view of the author's use of scatological humor in connection with the

Devil's minions which will be discussed later in this chapter. Mankind uses another apostrophe after the address to the soul. The second is addressed to the Virgin Mary:

> Lady, helpe! Souerens, yt doth my soull myche yll
> To se þe flesch prosperouse and þe soull trodyn
> > wnder fote.
> I xall go to yondyr man and asay [appeal to] hym I
> > wyll.
> I trust of gostly [spiritual] solace wyll be my bote.
> > (ll. 205-08)

The appeal to the Virgin is immediately followed by another apostrophe directed at the audience (*Sourens*), which indicates the level of Mankind's distress over the situation and brings the audience directly into the action once again. The next two lines indicate a course of action. The use of "I wyll" at the end of the line repeats "I xall" at the beginning (epanalepsis). Even though "wyll" and "xall" are not exactly the same word, they can be construed as such in this context. This rhetorical device emphasizes Mankind's resolve to get help from this unknown man (Mercy). The last line indicates a belief that Mercy will be his helper ("bote"), an irony that would not be wasted on the audience. Mercy's appearance may even be the answer to Mankind's prayer in line 205. Believing that Mercy can help him achieve spiritual comfort, which is actually allowing God to have total sovereignty over his soul, Mankind hails Mercy:

> All heyll, semely father! ȝe be welcom to þis house.
> Of þe very wysdom ȝe haue partycypacyon.
> My body wyth my soull ys euer querulose.
> I prey yow, for sent charyte, of yowr supportacyon.
> > (ll. 209-12)

In the context of an allegorical morality play, Mercy is exactly what Mankind needs in order to achieve spiritual solace. In such an environment, then, the word "house" may symbolize the body wherein the soul resides. At the moment there is unrest in the household because the soul "ys ever querulose" with the body. Mercy is not only welcome but essential to the satisfactory resolution of the problem. Mankind's whole speech could almost be classified as a form of mempsis in which the speaker makes his complaint and asks for help (Joseph 391). Mankind complains not about a specific person but about his own condition in which his body wars with his soul and seems to be winning. Mankind requests help from the Virgin Mary and then from Mercy to whom he states his plea three times, each becoming stronger, which is the rhetorical technique called graditio or climax:

> I trust of gostly solace
> (1. 208)
> ...
> I prey yow, for sent charyte,
> (1. 212)
> ...
> I beseche yow hertyle
> (1. 213)

The first is an indirect plea in the form of a belief that Mercy will help. The second begins with a pleading for the sake of holy charity, which is the rhetorical device known as deesis (Joseph 391). The third comes immediately after the second plea and is the strongest of all: "I beseche yow hertyle," which is also a phrase that echoes throughout the play—spoken by different characters—and provides a connecting thread. The cumulative effect of these three pleas is to emphasize the intensity of Mankind's distress. Such distress makes him a prime candidate to fall under the Devil's spell in this diabolical game, a fact of which Mankind seems to be aware as he says:

> I beseeche yow hertyly of yowr gostly comforte.
> I am onstedfast in lywynge; any name ys
>   Mankynde.
> My gostly enmy þe Deull wyll haue a grett
>   dyssporte
> In synfull gydynge [conduct] yf he may se me ende.
>   (11. 213-16)

Mankind recognizes his own weakness—"onstedfast in lywynge." Mankind needs Mercy's support to prevent the Devil from destroying him forever, which is the ultimate result of luring Mankind into sinful conduct and away from God's sovereignty. Mercy exhibits sympathy and understanding for Mankind's position when he acknowledges the battle between the body and the soul for sovereignty: "The temptacyon of þe flesch ȝe must resyst lyke a man, / For þer ys ever a batell betwyx þe soul and þe body" (11. 22627). The body-soul sovereignty motif is picked up by Mercy in the last scene, thus providing a connecting thread for the parts of the play, as Mercy points out the meaning of "flesch": "The flesch, þat ys þe vnclene concupissens [desires] of your body" (1. 887). Mercy then uses the rhetorical device commoratio in which the idea that one must allow the soul to rule over the desires of the body or risk losing that soul is repeated in different ways, exposing different facets of this notion:

> absteyne fro syn euermore after þis.
> ȝe may both saue and spyll [destroy] ȝowr sowle þat
>   ys so precyus.

> Libere well, libere nole God may not deny iwys
> [certainly]
> ...
> Of your synfull delectacion [delight] þat grewyth
> [grieves] your gostly substans [soul].
> ȝour body ys your enemy; let hym not have hys
> wyll.
>
> (ll. 892-97)

The Latin phrase (l. 894) reinforces the idea that Mankind must choose. God will not deny him. Man must abstain from sin and not allow his body to rule his soul if he is going to preserve his soul from damnation.

Another image the playwright uses to strengthen the sovereignty theme from a different perspective appears in Mercy's last speech in the first scene. Mercy uses the rhetorical technique of exemplum to incorporate a reference to Job into his advice to Mankind in order to depict how far the limits of humanity can be stretched to resist temptation:

> ȝe may not haue yowr intent at yowr fyrst dysyere.
> Se þe grett pacyence of Job in tribulacyon:
> Lyke as þe smyth trieth ern in þe feere,
> So was he triede by Godys vysytacyon.
> He was of yowr nature and of yowr fragylyte;
> Folow þe steppys of hym, my own swete son.
>
> (ll. 285-90)

Mercy uses the simile comparing Job's trials to the test of iron in a fire to point up the fact that God tests his people to make them stronger and better, a fact noted in the Bible. Job himself says that when he is tested by God, he will emerge as gold (Job 23:10). Job suffered much, but he did not question God's sovereignty. The allusion to Job underscores the notion that Mankind's human limits are much broader than he can imagine and offers hope that he will withstand the onslaught, giving the victory in this game to God. Mercy also quotes a Latin prayer (1. 292) to Mankind that Mercy ascribes to Job and encourages Mankind to use in time of trouble, as Job did. The Latin prayer translates as follows: "The Lord gives, the Lord takes away, as He wishes, thus it is. May the name of the Lord be blessed." This prayer emphasizes God's power and the need to submit to it as the right way, and, by comparing Mankind to Job, Mercy is both directly and indirectly exhorting Mankind to submit to the sovereignty of God, thereby shoring up the sovereignty theme from two directions at one time. In addition to support for the sovereignty theme, the allusion to Job also indicates the intended symbolic nature of the scatological humor, a notion which will be discussed in detail later in this chapter.

Still another image that the author uses to expose another dimension to the sovereignty theme is the horse-master image. As has been Mercy's inclination throughout the play, he sums up the message of his speech (11. 22644), which is basically to practice moderation in all things, in a proverb at the end of his speech:

> Yf a man haue an hors and kepe hym not to hye,
> He may then reull hym at hys own dysyere.
> If he be fede ouerwell he wyll dysobey.
> Ande in happe cast his master in þe myre.
> (11. 241–44)

As an example of Mercy's rhetorical virtuosity, this proverb is an absolute gem. The very nature of a proverb invokes the figure significatio, which is simply to imply more than is actually said. The proverb gives additional strength to Mercy's words stressing the importance of moderation by displaying another facet of the consequences of overindulgence. A pampered horse is not reliable and can be dangerous. The theme of sovereignty is emphasized in the relationship between horse and master. Symbolically, the horse represents Mankind, whose overindulgence in the sensual pleasures of the world can cause him to throw off his master (God), thereby fleeing the wise sovereignty of God to establish his own sovereignty over himself, creating a moral vacuum into which the Devil can easily move. Mercy's speech that ends with the horse proverb occurs during the episode in which Mankind laments the struggle going on between his body and soul. The last two lines of the horse proverb can be extended to include the body-soul dichotomy in the context of the sovereignty theme: "Yf he befede ouerwell he wyll dysobey / Ande in happe cast his master in þe myre." The ideal situation features the wisdom of the soul in command of the sensual desires of the body; however, overindulgence in the material and salacious things of the world will cause the body to throw off the soul. The image of the soul as the master lying in the "myre" graphically illustrates the dirt and filth that attaches itself to the soul when the flesh gains the upper hand in their continuous battle for supremacy, a notion that is reflected in the scatological humor sprinkled throughout the play. According to Sister Coogan the horse-rider metaphor representing the body-soul dichotomy is a commonplace in the medieval religious literature, and the rider (soul) must be responsible for guiding the horse (body) in this situation (29). The author thus intertwines two of his images in support of the sovereignty theme to achieve additional depth for his message.

Sister Miriam Joseph points out that Gorgias recommends using jesting to destroy an opponent's earnestness (373), which is the method New Gyse employs in an effort to diffuse the impact of the horse proverb. He uses the proverb in a much less dignified context than Mercy's and includes scatological humor to divert attention from the seriousness of Mercy's words. New Gyse also ties the horse image to the husband-wife image used earlier in the play (11. 135–39) to introduce the sovereignty theme:

> ȝe sey trew, ser, ȝe are no faytour.
> I haue fede my wyff so well tyll sche ys my master.
> I have a grett wonde on my hede, lo! and þeron leyth
> > a playster,
> Ande anoþer þer I pysse my peson.
> Ande my wyf were yowr hors, sche wolde yow all
> > to-banne.
>
> (11. 245–49)

Using Mercy's proverb, New Gyse compares his wife, whom he has treated far too well, to the overfed horse. She, too, resorts to violence and beats New Gyse to assert her sovereignty. Neither the horse nor the wife will obey her proper ordained master any longer. This reference to domestic sovereignty in both the house and the stable links these two images and reminds the audience of the major theme of the play, God's sovereignty over Mankind.

Mercy ends his deliberative oration with one last warning, which includes an allusion to the horse metaphor and a blessing for both Mankind and the audience:

> Yf ȝe dysples Gode, aske mercy anon,
> Ellys Myscheff wyll be redy to brace yow in hys
> > brydyll.
> Kysse me now, my dere darynge. Gode schelde yow
> > from yowr fon!
>
> (11. 305–07)

...

> The blessynge of God be wyth vow and wyth all þes
> worschyppull men!
>
> (1. 309)

Mercy thus warns Mankind that if he "displeases God" then Mischief will be ready to put a bridle on him. The metaphorical reference to Mankind as a horse and Mischief as the master underscores the sovereignty theme by graphically depicting the consequences of throwing off God's sovereignty. The use of the horse metaphor connects with Mercy's proverb and provides continuity and cohesion for the scene. By pronouncing a blessing (eulogia) on Mankind and the audience, Mercy pulls the audience into the action once again and identifies them with Mankind. The implication is that they, too, should heed Mercy's advice and be persuaded of the need to submit to God's sovereignty.

Titivillus also engages the horse metaphor when he enters in the second scene:

> ȝe þat haue goode hors, to yow I sey caueatis
> [beware]!
> Here ys an abyll felyschyppe to tryse [snatch] hem
> out at your gatys.
>
> (11. 476–77)

Titivillus labels the rogues, who are horse thieves, as an "abyll felyschyppe". Not only is this label an apt description of the worthless villains, but it becomes a connecting device when Titivillus repeats his warning in exactly the same words (11. 490–91) and when Mercy tells Mankind to flee "that felyschyppe" in line 726. The rhetorical device in which one attaches a label or an attribute to someone that later becomes important or relevant is called prolepsis. The reference to the group as an "abyll felyschyppe" takes on greater significance in the context of the horse metaphor established by Mercy's proverb (11. 241-44). This warning is, therefore, both literal in that the rogues will steal whatever they can and symbolic in that the horse symbolizes Mankind's soul, the object of this game with God. As a group New Gyse, Nowadays, and Nought are quite accomplished in the art of temptation and are quite capable of cheating in the game if their powers of rhetorical persuasion are insufficient to entice Mankind into sin. The implication of the warning seems to be that New Gyse and his friends will snatch Mankind's soul from Mercy's influence and pull Mankind into the jaws of temptation and sin.

The rhetorical technique that the playwright employs to depict Mercy's reaction to Mankind's apparent decision to throw off God's sovereignty and follow the Devil is similar to that of graditio in which Mercy's emotions range from useless lamentation to a specific course of action. Although parallel construction is absent, the emotions build from the numbness of lament to anger to pity to defense and, finally, to a resolve to win Mankind back from Mischief and his friends. Mercy's speech in the third scene takes on the form of the figure threnos in its first eight lines as he laments Mankind's unfortunate behavior:

> My mynde ys dyspersyde [distracted], my body
>   trymmelyth as þe aspen leffe.
> The terys xuld trekyll down by my chekys, were not
>   yowr reuerrence [due respect].
> Yt were to me solace, þe cruell vysytacyon of deth.
> Wythout rude behauer I kan not expresse þis
>   inconvenyens.
> Wepynge, sythynge, and sobbynge were my
>   suffycyens [sustenance];
> All naturall nutriment to me as caren ys odybull

[hateful].
My inwarde afflixcyon ȝeldyth me tedyouse wnto
yowr presens.
I kan not bere yt ewynly þat Mankynde ys so
flexybull.

(11. 734–41)

To set the stage for his lament, Mercy uses the simile comparing himself to an aspen leaf that trembles in the wind. Both Mercy's mind and his body are shaken and disoriented by Mankind's refusal to obey God and by Mankind's becoming a member of the opposition. Mercy is overcome by emotion, weeping and sighing. His wonderful gift with words fails him, because words seem inadequate to the task of describing his grief. Metaphorically, tears and sighs become Mercy's only food ("suffyeyns"). Juxtaposing a simile next to the food metaphor, Mercy describes real food as being as hateful to him as dead flesh ("caren"). This simile takes on additional meaning in the context of a lement. Mankind's behavior will result in his becoming "caren" with no hope of eternal life; therefore, the word "caren" literally refers to a corpse and figuratively to Mankind, which is a clever way to point up the consequences of failure to accept God's sovereignty. Mercy says that his inward pain brings him "tedyouse" ("dully") into Mankind's presence (1. 740). The word "tedyouse" following the description of pain and anguish indicates that Mercy is numb and in a state of shock. The last line of the lament shows a return of a spark of life which ignites into anger that "Mankynde ys so flexybull." Mercy moves from emotional lamentation into anger, tying the two parts together by a pun on "Mankind" and "Man onkynd":

I kan not bere yt ewynly þat Mankynde ys so
flexybull.

> Man onkynde, whereuer þou be!
>
> (ll. 741-42)

This pun ties into the same sort of pun in the first scene when Mercy leaves Mankind alone with the rogues and offers a last note of warning and concern:

> Thynke well in yowr hert, yowr name ys
>   Mankynde;
> Be not wnkynde to Gode, I prey yow be hys
>   seruante.
>
> (ll. 279-80)

These puns form a structural connecting device, as well as pointing up the fact that Mankind does not have Mercy's teachings firmly enough in his heart to prevent temptation from overcoming his basic desire to be God's servant. The apostrophe to "Man onkynde" in this speech initiates an angry tirade against ungrateful Mankind. This angry portion of the speech is a form of onedismus in which the speaker upbraids someone for his ingratitude or impiety (Joseph 392). By repeating the same idea with different shades of meaning (commoratio), Mercy emphasizes the restrictive aspects of sin: "To dyscharge þin orygynall offence, thraldam, and captyuyte" (l. 743). Mankind's sin enslaves him as a thrall and as a captive. The "orygynall offence" refers to Adam's sin, but it also refers to the fact that Mankind has committed a second offence by refusing God sovereignty over his life. Without God as his Sovereign Lord, Mankind will once again be enslaved by the Devil. Although the speech is a monologue and Mankind is not present, Mercy continues to chastise Mankind for his ingratitude, pointing out that Christ has shed his blood to purge Mankind of sin. Mercy despairs over Mankind's "mutabylyte" and engages in a rhetorical question geared to further chide the hapless Mankind (epiplexis) and to illustrate Mercy's difficulty in understanding how Mankind could have ignored all of Mercy's teachings: "Why are þou so oncurtess, so inconsyderatt? Alasse, who [woe] ys me!" (1. 748). The simile in line 749 graphically displays Mankind's inconstancy: "As þe fane [weathervane] / þat turnyth wyth þe wynde, so þou art conuertyble." The wind that turns Mankind seems to be a rhetorical wind, because he turns in the direction of whomever he talked with last. Mercy uses a proverb to illustrate how foolish he has been to believe Mankind: "In trust ys treson; þi promes ys not credyble" (1. 750). By trusting Mankind Mercy gave him the power to commit treason. The word "treson" connotes disloyalty to one's king or government. In this situation the word supports the sovereignty theme, because there could be no treason if Mankind had been loyal to his king— God. A trust has been broken and loyalty shifted to another. In the context of the game metaphor the opposition now controls the ball. The reference to God and his Holy Court harks back to the mock manor court (11. 664-725) when Mankind officially changes sides, and forms a connecting thread: "To God and to all þe holy corte of hewyn þou art despectyble" (1. 752). To illustrate just how despicable Mankind is to God and heaven, Mercy uses a Latin poem as an exemplum, which translates as follows: "Law and nature, Christ and all loves / They damn the ungrateful, they weep for him who was born outside" (11. 754-55). After this poem damning the ungrateful, Mercy moves from his anger into pity, using vehement supplication (deesis) to the Virgin Mary along with apostrophe to beg for pity and compassion for Mankind: "O goode Lady and Moþer of mercy, haue pety and compassyon / Of þe wrechydnes of Mankynde, þat ys so wanton and so frayll!" (11. 756-57). This supplication to the Virgin is a form of the figure medela, which is a kind of apology for the obvious and irrefutable sins of our friends. Mercy then moves from pathos to defense of Mankind's actions much as a parent would do for his son. The son is not really at fault; it is the bad company that he keeps that is to blame: "New Gyse, Nowadays, Nought wyth þer allectuose ways / They haue pervertyde Mankynde, my swet sun, I haue well espyede [perceived]" (11. 762-63). Mercy resolves to get Mankind back from those cursed villains and away from their materialistic lifestyle:

> A wyth þes cursyde caytyfs [villains], and I may
> [if I can help it], he xall not long indure.
> I, Mercy, hys father gostly, wyll procede forth and
> do my propyrte [special attribute].
> Lady, helpe! þis maner of lyuynge ys a detestabull
> plesure.
>
> (11. 764-66)

Mercy calls on the Virgin for help (deesis) in his plan to wrest Mankind from the forces of evil. Curiously Mercy ends line 766 with an oxymoron, "detestabull plesure." Possibly Mercy recognizes the allure of the sensual way of living and the "fun" that it produces for Mankind; yet that "fun" evolving from music, alcohol, and barmaids can quickly deteriorate into criminal behavior, as the example of Mischief and his friends illustrates. Such things are detestable to God and dishonor Him. Mercy is determined now to win Mankind back to God's fold and goes in search of him.

The playwright has carefully employed numerous rhetorical figures and techniques in constructing *Mankind* on the game metaphor, a method for which the tradition of sinister comedy provides literary precedent. The forces of Good and Evil, represented by Mercy and Mischief, each seek to win Mankind's soul through the persuasive power of rhetoric. The playwright skillfully uses his imagery to display various aspects of the two major themes, sovereignty and rhetoric, and subtly builds Mercy's ethos, an important aspect of his rhetorical ability, throughout the play. The primary images— the horse proverb, the husband-wife image, the body-soul image— fold over each other as they support the sovereignty and rhetoric themes, a technique which permits support from several angles at one time. The corn metaphor and the motifs of Christian doctrine support the themes and provide connecting links for the parts of the play. The author fits every minute piece of *Mankind* securely into the overall structure.

A Rhetorical Analysis of *Mankind*

Part Two

In addition to the sovereignty theme, the second major theme in *Mankind* is the theme of rhetoric, or the importance of language, which the playwright adroitly intertwines with the sovereignty theme to strengthen both the meaning and the structure of the play. The theme of rhetoric permeates the play in both direct and indirect references to language and the quality of its usage. One of the first instances illustrating Mercy's awareness of his rhetorical expertise occurs in his encounter with Mischief in the first scene: "Avoyde, goode broþer! ȝe ben culpable / To interrupte thus my talkyng delectable" (11. 64–65). Mercy chastises Mischief for interrupting his "delectable" speech, which indicates that Mercy might have been a bit carried away by his own flights of rhetoric until Mischief brought him down with his mockery. Mischief's own response to Mercy's criticism is irrelevant to the situation: "Ser, I haue noþer horse nor sadyll, / Therefor I may not ryde" (11. 66–67). Such a response is inappropriate and is a vice of language (heterogenium) related to sophism (Joseph 300), Mischief's second such error in this episode, which forms an implicit contrast to Mercy's "delectable" speech. Another reference to language usage appears after Nought tells Mercy that he had heard Mercy call the three of them, just as New Gyse and Nowadays chime in, describing their activities at the time Mercy supposedly called them. Mercy is impressed with the rhetorical exhibition of the three rogues and says, "Few wordys, few and well sett!" (1. 102) to which New Gyse responds:

> Ser, yt ys þe new gyse and þe new jett [custom].
> Many wordys and schortely sett.
> Thys ys þe new gyse, every-dele [euery bit].
> (11. 103–05)

A connection is therefore established early in the play between rhetoric and the "new fashion" ("new gyse"), which underscores the notion that the playwright was aware of the value of craftsmanship in his play. *Mankind*, a late fifteenth-century play, reflects in the language of the villainous characters the rhetorical fashion of the day, which was prolix speaking (Smart, "Some Notes on *Mankind*" 113). As Smart points out, the three villains are defending the new style in language ("Some Notes on *Mankind*" 113), just as they are defending the new style of living, which is idle and unproductive, emphasizing sensual pleasure rather than honest work. The villains not only represent the new way of living but also the new way of speaking and writing, whereas Mercy represents the traditional way of living under God's sovereignty and of speaking well-chosen words eloquently united and founded on wisdom. New Gyse's words connecting rhetoric to the new fashion convey the same idea as the words of Nought in the second scene. In this scene Nought tires of playing the flute and asks if his friends have collected the money from the audience: "I sey New Gyse, Nowadays: Estis vos pecuniatus? [are you in the money?]" (1. 471). This line, according to Eccles, is to be translated: "I speak in the new fashion" (221nM471). These two speeches of New Gyse and Nought, therefore, form a connecting link in the play and stress the importance of language. Nought's use of Latin as the "new fashion" mocks Mercy's frequent use of Latin and perhaps Mischief's bungled Latin, as well. Nought is not too shy to ridicule his cohort's speech habits, if given the opportunity. In the context of the collection episode the reference to the new fashion in language creates an indirect tie to the materialistic new fashion in living which revolves around money, thereby making the collection scene itself an important symbolic element of the play. Later in the play Mischief appears in broken fetters and describes a scene of murder, debauchery, and theft as part of his escape from prison, pointing out in the last two lines of his speech that the new device for getting money ("chesance") fares well in his eyes: "Here ys anow [enough] for me; be of goode chere! / ȝet well fare þe new chesance!" (11. 648-49). The implication here is that the old way is to work for money, whereas the new way is to rob and kill for it. Mischief's situation illustrates just what is involved when one decides to follow the "new fashion." The connection established between language and the new fashion in living extends to the new way of getting money as well. The implication may be that the new rhetorical fashion does not have a sound moral foundation.

Another episode marking the importance of language in this play takes place after Mankind is brainwashed by Titivillus's rhetoric and wants to join with the rogues. New Gyse wants to write Mankind's name in Mischief's book: "Master Myscheff, we wyll yow exort [beseech] / Mankyndys name in yowr bok for to report" (1. 662). Once the name is actually written down, Mankind will be theirs; however, Mischief decides that holding a manor court will be a better way to initiate Mankind into their ranks. Mischief appoints Nought as the steward who is to record the proceedings. An exchange ensues among Mischief, Nowadays, and Nought as his friends admire Nought's handwriting:

> NOUGHT: Holde, master Myscheff, and rede þis.
> MYSCHEFF: Here ys blottibus in blottis, Blottorum blottibus istis. I beschrew yowr erys, a fayer hande!
> NOWADAYS: ȝe, yt ys a goode rennynge fyst [cursive hand]. Such an hande may not be myst.
> NOUGHT: I xulde haue don better, hade I wyst [known].
> (11. 679–85)

After this exchange of praise and false modesty on the part of Nought, Mischief reads the manor role to the group (11. 687–93), during the course of which reading Mischief inserts a reference to Nought as he records the proceedings and a comparison of him to Tully: "As Nought hath wrytyn; here ys owr Tulli" (1. 692). The concentration on the act of writing emphasizes the theme of the importance of language and how it is used. Where it is intelligible at all, the Latin that Nought uses is gibberish and fractured Latin. Much is made of Nought's handwriting, placing emphasis on how it looks rather than on what is said, which can be construed as a vote for pretty words and empty rhetoric. The comparison of Nought to "Tulli," whom most critics agree is a reference to Cicero (Eccles 225nM692), strengthens the theory that rhetoric is an important motif in the play and that the author is aware of the skills involved in good rhetorical technique. Of course, Cicero was a lawyer and in the context of a mock manor court that comparison is also a possibility; however, the thrust of the episode is how well Nought is recording the events. Thus the comparison seems to be with Cicero's outstanding ability with words and with his genius at putting them together. Irony results from the contrast between the greatest Roman rhetorician and this uneducated derelict who knows very little if any Latin.

The jacket that Mankind receives after the proceedings has many symbolic meanings, and some of these meanings appear to give subtle and oblique support to the rhetoric theme. During this mock manor court New Gyse notices Mankind's long robe and wants to convert it into a jacket: "I promyst yow a fresch [gay] jakett after þe new gyse [fashion]" (1. 676). Nought's writing of the proceedings interrupts this jacket episode, creating a delay. After the delay, Nowadays grows anxious: "What how, Neu Gyse! / þou makyst moche taryynge. / þat jakett xall not be worth a ferthynge" (11. 694–95). The new fashion is such a fleeting and shallow notion that within the space of a few minutes the new fad or new jacket can become outmoded and unfashionable, and therefore useless. Symbolically, the line refers to the useless chase of material things which soon wear out or are outdated. Implicit in the line is the contrast with Mercy's traditional doctrine, which is solid and never goes out of fashion. After the delay, New Gyse returns with the jacket, but Nought is horrified at the result, complaining bitterly about its poor shape and heavy weight. Feeling responsible for the coat, Nought takes it away to repair it. The ritual initiation ensues while Nought is gone. He returns after the initiation ritual with a short jacket considered handsome by New Gyse:

> Yt ys a goode jake of fence [defense] for a mannys
> body.

Hay, doog, hay! Whoppe whoo! Go yowr wey
   lyghtly!
ȝe are well made for to ren [move rapidly].
                    (ll. 719–21)

The first jacket may symbolize the unbalanced and burdensome life led by these criminals, since it is cut poorly, is too heavy, and is shaped incorrectly. Nought remakes the jacket and New Gyse says that it is now a good defense for the body and remarks on one's ability to run in it. The diacope in which "hay" [run] is repeated separated only by "doog" ("dog") along with the exclamation "whoppe who" ("hurrah") draws attention to the line giving it added importance; therefore, one can see the implication of a lighter jacket made for one who must move quickly. The beginning of a life of crime is burdensome until one gets used to it and learns the methods. Then a burdensome life is altered to one of constant flight. Either way, Mankind's soul will never know peace while he wears that jacket. Since this episode weaves in and out of the mock manor court episode, which emphasizes the theme of rhetoric, this jacket may symbolize Mankind's conversion to the new fashion in living and, by extension, the new fashion in language. The jacket that Mankind receives may possibly be a reflection of the jacket Haukyn wears in *Piers the Plowman*. Scholars have already noted influences from *Piers* in *Mankind*. For instance, MacKenzie agrees with Keiller that "the agricultural episode in *Piers Plowman* is the source of the corresponding episode in *Mankind*," but MacKenzie disagrees with her that this episode in *Piers* is the source for the entire play ("A New Source for *Mankind* " 98). Keiller believes that the central motive, the characters, and the action in *Mankind* come from *Piers* (355). MacKenzie seems to be more nearly correct in his assessment that *Piers* is an influence rather than an actual source as Keiller suggests. The possibility that Mankind's jacket is a variation of Haukyn's jacket stained with sin lends support to Mackenzie's influence theory. Mankind's long robe is changed into a short jacket symbolic of his new position in life. The two coats are graphic symbols of the lifestyles led by the men who wear them. Haukyn in Book VIII of the B-Text of *Piers Plowman*, p. 161, talks about revenging himself through the power of his tongue when his musclemen cannot extract vengeance through physical violence:

> Haukyn's tongue was always ready to wrangle; and
> he would repeat all the ill that he knew of others,
> accusing men behind their backs and praying for
> their destruction. Whatever he heard about Will, he
> would tell to Walter, and whatever Walter told him,
> he repeated to Will; and his evil-speaking turned
> even his best friends into enemies. "I revenge
> myself," he said, "by the power of the tongue, if I
> can't do it by other men's muscles; and if I fail, I
> chafe and fret like a rusty pair of shears."

The fact that Haukyn cheats, steals, kills, and values material things above the spiritual puts him in the camp of Mischief and his friends. Haukyn also engages in the lies and idle language used by the Devil's minions to win Mankind. The implication in Haukyn's speech that words are powerful weapons reflects the theme of the importance of language in *Mankind* and strengthens the belief that Haukyn may have been an influence on the author when he created the mock court episode. A parallel exists between the two men in that Mankind, after his ritual initiation into the group, has both a jacket and specific directions to behave in the same manner that Haukyn behaves in *Piers Plowman*. Mankind's new jacket now represents the idle language engaged in by both his new peer group and by Haukyn, as well as their disreputable lifestyles.

Mercy, of course, has nothing but disdain for such idle words. Mercy views the new fashion so boldly practiced by New Gyse, Nowadays, and Nought as empty rhetoric and idle language that present a threat to Mankind's soul. The first opportunity that Mercy gets to voice his displeasure with the sort of language used by the rogues occurs after Nought makes his obscene remarks about Pope Pokett (ll. 143–46): "Thys idyll language ȝe xall repent. / Out of þis place I wield ȝe went" (ll. 147–48). Thus, Mercy is as quick to criticize faulty language as he is to compliment the good rhetorical techniques of "Few wordys, few and well sett!" in line 102. New Gyse responds to Mercy's criticism with another direct but sarcastic reference to rhetoric: "Goo we hens all thre wyth on assent. / My fadyr ys yrke [weary] of owr eloquence" (ll. 149-50). Mercy again subtly points to the importance of language and the unreliability of appearance in his last words of warning to Mankind at the end of the first scene:

> Be ware of New Gyse, Nowadays, and Nought
> Nyse in þer aray, in language þei be large,
> To perverte yowr condycyons all þe menys xall be
>   sowte.
>
>   (ll. 293–95)

The word "large" translates as "licentious," which Mercy would consider to be "idle language." The fellows dress well ("Nyse in þer aray."), a fact which circumspectly warns of the deception involved in external appearance. The chiasmus used in the construction of this line and the alliteration of [n] carried through from line 293 focus attention on the message and increase its importance. A veiled warning of unfair tactics in the game can be seen in the word "menys" in the last line of the quotation. The *Middle English Dictionary* does not list "menys" as such, but "menis" is listed as a form of "menace," which means "the act of threatening or fact of being threatened" (118). The line then translates: "To perverte your habits all the menace shall be sought." This translation does not conform with modern grammatical standards, but the negative connotations of "menace" include the possibility of illegal means. The word "menys" would better serve modern grammatical standards if it translated as "means," but there are no such provisions in the *Middle English Dictionary*. If the line were translated using "means" instead of "menace," the impact would be lost because means has the connotations of legality in this context. Titivillus embodies the idea of "menace" because he goes beyond the boundaries of the rules of the game rather than seeking all available "means" within the rules to win.

Mischief, New Gyse, Nowadays, and Nought are not as adept at the art of language as Mercy is, and they have neither wisdom nor truth on their side as he has; therefore, the villains resort to rhetorical maneuvers to soften the impact of Mercy's words. Mischief initiated this strategy at the beginning of the play after Mercy's opening speech, which displayed the kind of opposition the villains could expect in this game. Mischief decides to use Mercy's own speech habits and techniques to ridicule him and to make Mercy's teachings seem ridiculous and ludicrous. Mischief's ridicule begins with the corn metaphor and Mercy's tendency to use Latin maxims. New Gyse, Nowadays, and Nought are not in the same league with Mischief with regard to language manipulation, but they follow his lead in the strategy to mock and belittle Mercy, hoping to discredit him with Mankind. New Gyse attempts to downplay Mercy's considerable ability with language with a mocking retort to Mercy's remark that New Gyse has "but a lytyll favour in my communycacyon" (1. 123): "Ey, ey! Yowr body is full of Englysch Laten. / I am aferde yt wyll brest" (11. 124–25). Mischief overhears Mercy's resolution to find Mankind after his defection to the other side and Mercy's cries of "Mankind, vbi es?" Seizing another opportunity to step on Mercy's eloquent language, Mischief says:

> My prepotent [especially powerful] fader, when ȝe
>> sowpe [sup], sowpe owt [drink up] yowr messe
>> [portion].
> ȝe are all to-gloryede [puffed up greatly] in yowr
>> termys; ȝe make many a lesse [falsehood].
> Wyll ȝe here [listen]? He cryeth euer 'Mankynde,
>> vbi es?'
>
> (11. 772–74)

The initial phrase, "My prepotent fader," is a mocking reply to Mercy's "My predylecte [especially beloved] son" in the previous line (771), which sets up the mocking tone for the speech following Mercy's lament at Mankind's tractability. In the context of a taunting speech the two clauses at the end of this first line are almost a proverb: "when ȝe sowpe, sowpe owt yowr messe." The repetition of "sowpe" (anadiplosis) emphasizes the idea of drinking up one's portion, which symbolically means accepting what one is given. Mercy chose to participate in this game, but now that Mankind has changed sides and Mercy is losing, he is unhappy and full of lamentation. Mischief is pointing out in proverbial fashion, a favored rhetorical technique of Mercy's, that one accepts what he is given, if he sits down to eat. The last two lines complain of Mercy's extravagant vocabulary, accuse him of lying, and exhibit mimesis in the imitation of Mercy's cries. New Gyse falls in with Mercy's speech in the same mocking tone used by Mischief:

> Hic hyc, hic hic, hic hic, hic hic!
> þat ys to sey, here, here, here! ny dede in þe cryke.

Yf ӡe wyll haue hym, goo and syke, syke, syke!
Syke not ouerlong, for losynge of yowr mynde!
(ll. 775-78)

Feigning an answer to Mercy's "Vbi es?" New Gyse uses epizeuxis by repeating "hic" without other words intervening (Joseph 307). New Gyse then employs expergesis to insert and explain further (Joseph 295) by using the phrase "þat ys to sey" before translating "hic" into English and continuing the repetition. This exuberance mocks Mercy's use of English and Latin along with his repetition of the question, a fine job of mimesis on the part of a rogue. Going a bit further, New Gyse offers advice rather than criticism; however, that advice is couched in mocking terms with the repetition of "syke" (epizeuxis) in line 777. The use of anadiplosis with the repetition of "syke," which ends line 777, initially in line 778 changes the mocking advice into a warning not to search very long for sanity's sake. The implication is that Mankind is so fully in the villain's grasp that Mercy will not find him, but underlying the bold warning may be the fear that if Mercy searches and does find Mankind, Mercy's powers of persuasion will wrest Mankind from the Devil's side. Nowadays soon gets into the act with his comrades by taunting Mercy with the idea that Mankind may be a criminal and to see him Mercy will have to get himself arrested: If ӡe wyll have Mankynde, how domine, domine, dominus! / ӡe must speke to þe schryue [sheriff] for a cape corpus [writ of arrest]" (ll. 779-80).

The villains realize that Mercy will probably regain Mankind, if he ever finds him. They are forced to devise a plan to forestall Mercy or the game is lost; therefore, Mischief calls for "a parlement" (l. 787) to decide on a course of action. New Gyse has a plan: "Myscheff, go sey to hym þat Mercy sekyth eurywere. / He wyll honge hymselff, I wndyrtake [venture to say] for fere" (ll. 792-93). New Gyse believes that Mankynde will die rather than face Mercy.

If Mankind dies while still on the rogues's side, they win the game, because Mercy's rhetoric is useless at that point, and he can never regain Mankind after death. Mischief likes the plan and points out how well New Gyse said it: "I assent þerto; yt ys wyttyly seyde and well" (1. 794). The line strengthens the notion of the power of the word. Mischief's distress, illustrated by his frantic screaming for "a parlement" when he learns that Mercy looks for Mankind, is relieved by New Gyse's soothing words offering a solution. So great is his relief that Mischief remarks on New Gyse's rhetorical ability. Mischief's nervousness results from his fear of the power of Mercy's words. Death will separate Mankind from Mercy's "to gloryede termys" (1. 773). One critic has pointed out that the rogues are perverting God's word when they use words similar to those used by Mercy and that this method is the way the author dramatizes "Mankind's disregard of God's word" (Ashley 141). Mischief's fear is obviously a well-founded one. Nowadays praises New Gyse's plan: "All þe bokys in þe worlde, yf þei hade be wndon [opened], / Kowde not a cownselde ws bett [advised us better]" (11. 797-98). Books are the ultimate collection of words and, therefore, a source of power. Nowadays is impressed with New Gyse's rhetoric and persuaded that this plan is the best available. Mischief and his companions put the plan into action with New Gyse providing an actual demonstration of the proper way to hang oneself: "Lo, Mankynde! do as I do; þis ys þi new gyse. / Gyff [put] þe roppe just to þy neke; þis ys myn avyse [advice]" (11. 804-05). This speech is symbolic because by imitating the new fashion represented by New Gyse, Mankind symbolically chooses a path that leads to death. This episode is a concrete depiction of Mankind's action and its consequences, a creative touch illustrating the wages of sin far better than the sermon of any priest. Mercy arrives in the nick of time and drives the villains away with a rod reminiscent of Mankind's driving them off with his spade in the first scene. With Mercy's arrival New Gyse's friends run away, leaving him dangling with the rope on his neck:

> Qweke, qweke, qweke! Alass, my thrott! I beschrew
> yow, mary [indeed]!
> A, Mercy, Chrystys coppyde [heaped-up] curse go
> wyth yow, and Sent Dauy [St. David]!
> Alasse, my wesant [throat]! ʒe were sumwhat to
> nere.
>
> (11. 808-10)

The repetition of "qweke" (epizeuxis), the sound of choking, ties into the episode in which New Gyse relates his first near-hanging (11. 615-24). The last line of that speech is very similar to line 810 of this episode: "Alasse, how my neke ys sore, I make avowe!" (1. 624). Both episodes end with New Gyse complaining about his throat. Hanging him by the throat would close off the lies and the empty rhetoric, thereby imparting a symbolic aura to the emphasis on New Gyse's throat. The last speech (11. 808-10) is full of courses (ara), a technique which is appropriate. Having lost the game, or at least this round, to Mercy, all that is left is to toss useless curses at him. Lies, even when dressed in rhetorical frills, are no match for truth.

The mockery of Mercy's superior language skills continues when Nowadays asks Mercy to translate his obscene verse into Latin. Using a metaphor, Nowadays insinuates that Mercy's learning and his ability with words and languages involve trickery in which Mercy can just pull the needed words or information out of a bag like a magician: "Now opyn yowr sachell wyth Laten wordys / Ande sey me þis in clericall manere" (11. 133-34). These lines refer to translation of Nowadays's dirty little rhyme into Latin. The word "clerycall" can be translated as the word "subtle." This definition coupled with the image of words carried in a bag to be brought out at will just as a magician brings out his tricks indicates Nowadays's belief in Mercy's skills as a rhetorician and a translator. Disparagement of the skills as some sort of magic trick is an effort on Nowadays's part to undermine Mercy's ethos and to make his own lack of such skills seem less important than it really is; however, by ridiculing Mercy, who associates himself with Christ in the opening speech, Nowadays is indirectly mocking Christ and His Representatives, which could also include the clergy. Nowadays's companions's ridicule of Mercy falls into the same category. Although *Mankind* is a late medieval play, this rhetorical satire of the clergy reveals overtones of the Renaissance, since the first rumblings of rejection of clerical authority heralded the onset of that period (Miller, *Readings in Medieval Rhetoric* xv). If this notion is accepted, it is another indication of the literary sophistication of the author.

Along with the specific references, both stated and implied, to language and the quality of usage, Mercy and the representatives of the Devil who oppose him in this diabolical game for Mankind's soul each engage in certain rhetorical maneuvers designed to persuade Mankind to join their particular team. Some of these rhetorical techniques have been discussed briefly in the sections of this chapter dealing with the framework device, game metaphor, and the sovereignty theme. With regard to the rhetorical theme, these techniques require a more detailed discussion. For example, Mercy uses his verbal dexterity to set up a strong positive ethos in his opening speech, which is part of the framework device, which encloses the action of the play. Mercy continues to enhance that ethos during the play. In order to illustrate his genuine care and concern for Mankind's well being, Mercy substitutes patronyms for Mankind's proper name, a rhetorical figure called antonomasia, and arranges these patronyms in a climactic order throughout the speech (graditio), revealing an increasing tenderness and devotion:

> I have mocke care for yow, my own frende.
> (1. 277)
>
> ...
>
> Folow þe steppys of hym, my own swete son,
> (1. 290)
>
> ...
>
> Kysse me now, my dere darlynge
> (1. 307)

Such a technique subtly encourages Mankind to believe in Mercy's desire to protect him and to act positively on the advice offered in this deliberative speech. When Mankind enters the play in the first scene and cries out for help with his warring body and soul, Mercy uses the rhetorical device of paramythia in his response to Mankind's plea for help. Paramythia is a form of speech in which one offers comfort and encouragement in time of need. Mercy asks Christ's comfort for Mankind and encourages him to stand on his own feet, offering to help Mankind avoid evil:

> Cryst send yow good comforte! ȝe be welcum, my
> frende;
> Stonde wyppe on yowr fete, I prey yow aryse.
> My name ys Mercy; ȝe be to me full hende.
> To eschew vyce I will yow awyse.
> (11. 217-20)

Realizing the appeal that the sensual lifestyle of the three derelicts and Mischief might have for Mankind's fragile nature, Mercy continues his deliberative speech, reminding Mankind that life is short and that he must practice moderation in all things and serve God with all of his heart:

> Remember, my frende, þe tyme of contynuance.
> So helpe me Gode, yt ys but a chery tyme.
> Spende yt well; serue God wyth hertys affyance.
> Dystempure not yowr brayn wyth goode ale nor
>   wyth wyn.
> (11. 233-36)

Mercy heightens his emotional appeal to Mankind by the use of the oath (orcos), "So helpe me Gode," while simultaneously adding the weight of God's authority to his words. The metaphorical comparison of the length of life to the briefness of the cherry-harvest festival graphically underscores the urgency of the situation. Mercy wants desperately for Mankind to absorb the full impact of the message. Mercy engages in good rhetorical strategy by refusing to forbid Mankind the use of alcohol altogether and by stressing the notion of moderation through initial repetition of the word "Mesure" (anaphora), as he continues:

> Mesure ys tresure. Y forbyde yow not þe vse.
> Mesure yowrsylf euer; be ware of excesse
> þe syperfluouse gyse I wyll þat ȝe refuse,
> When nature ys suffysyde, anon þat ȝe sese [cease].
> (11. 237-40)

Mercy uses commoratio to gain strong emphasis for the idea of moderation in all things by repeating it in different words:

> Mesure ys tresure
> ...

> Mesure yowysylf euer; be ware of excesse.
> ...
> When nature ys suffysyde, anon þat ȝe sese.

Mercy, who has a tendency to sermonize as his initial speech illustrates, tries very hard to make his advice practical for Mankind, and for the audience, as well.

In addition to enhancing his ethos and making his doctrine attractive, Mercy uses his knowledge of rhetoric to make a subtle connection between the idle language of New Gyse and his companions and idle living in his second long speech in the first scene. Mercy's first speech has all the earmarks of a sermon, whereas this second long speech sounds much like a lawyer's opening remarks to a jury. He is alone and addressing the audience as in the opening speech. The first sentence sets the tone of the speech and aligns Mercy on God's side opposed to the "three disreputable guests," who have just left:

> Thankyde be Gode, we haue a fayer dylyuerance
> Of þes thre onthryfty [disreputable] gestys.
> They know full lytyll what ys þer ordynance.
> I preue by reson þei be wers þen bestys.
>   (11. 162-65)

Mercy sets up his argument by pointing out that these rascals do not know their appointed place ("ordynance"), meaning that they have overstepped the bounds of the behavior allotted to them in their place in the hierarchy of beings. The medieval audience would know this allusion and understand that God was at the top of the hierarchy, then the angels, followed by man and the beasts who occupy the position below man. Continuing in the forensic style of his speech, Mercy uses the refutative enthymeme to argue that in opposition to the accepted notion that men are better than beasts because of their higher place in the hierarchy of God's creations, some men do not understand their place in the natural order and violate the rules of their own natures, thus making these men worse than beasts:

> I preue by reson þei be wers þen bestys:
> A best doth after hys natural instytucyon;
> ȝe may conseyue [understand] by there dysporte
> [conduct] and behauour.
> þer joy ande delyte ys in derysyon [derision]
> Of her owyn Cryste to hys dyshonur.
> (11. 165-69)

The use of anadiplosis in which "bestys" at the end of line 165 is repeated in "A best" at the beginning of line 166 signals the enthymeme. Mercy points out that a beast behaves according to his natural ordained form (1. 166). The implication is that New Gyse and his cohorts do not behave according to their natural ordained form. In the context of Mercy's opening speech, which labeled God as Creator of all things, "natural instytucyon" translated as "natural ordained form" must refer to both beasts and men as creations or children of God. If one accepts "natural instytucyon" as referring to God-created entities, then natural behavior for such beings is to honor their creator, according to Mercy's logic; however, Mercy does not state this idea but points out the behavior of the three "onthryfty guests," which the audience has witnessed. Mercy then reminds the audience that the unsavory men take delight in ridiculing ("derysyon") "her own Chryste." The three villains have convicted themselves, and they are not even present. Mercy probably has the audience totally in sympathy with his position at this point; therefore, he makes examples of the absent defendants, using their behavior to warn the audience:

> Thys condycyon of leuying, yt ys prejudycyall;
> Be ware þerof, yt ys wers þan ony felony or treson.
> How may yt be excusyde befor þe Justyce of all
> When for euery ydyll worde we must ȝelde a reson?
> (11. 170-73)

Mercy thus issues a warning against idle language. Mercy gives this warning on good authority because according to Richards, based on his reading of Matthew and Mark, Jesus once said that " 'The things that come out of the mouth come from the heart, and these make a man 'unclean.' For out of the heart come evil thoughts, murder, adultery, sexual immorality, theft, false testimony, slander' " (254). The heart is considered to be the center of one's personality and the seat of human rebellion (Richards 254). Mercy, therefore, links one's language with the state of one's heart and soul, a notion which gives a great deal of power to the word. Mercy further points out in lines 172-73 that idle language will be difficult to justify before God: "How may yt be excusyde befor þe Justyce of all / when for every ydyll worde we must ȝelde a reson?"

In these two lines Mercy uses the figure called epiplexis in which a question is posed for the purpose of criticism or reproach rather than the purpose of acquiring information. This rhetorical question is particularly helpful at this point, because it is a positive way to state a very negative thing, and, as such it allows Mercy to impart the notion that the people in the audience must also be careful of their language without arousing the hostility of an accusation, which may often be the case with priests and their sermons.

Mercy follows up the message about the perils of empty, idle words with a more subtle message on physical idleness or an idle way of living:

> They haue grett ease, þerfor, þei wyll take no
>   thought.
> But how þen when þe angell of hewyn xall blow þe
>   trumpe
> Ande sey to þe transgressors þat wykkydly hath
>   wrought,
> 'Cum forth onto yowr Juge and ȝelde yowr
>   acownte?
>
>   (ll. 174–77)

The first line of this quotation sets up a new enthymeme and indirectly introduces the idea of honest toil as the preferred behavior, an idea which becomes a recurring motif in the play and is later symbolized by Mankind's spade. Mercy is pointing out that New Gyse, Nowadays, and Nought have too much time to play and do not think about the consequences of their actions. The implication is that honest work instead of idleness would occupy the villains' time productively. Idle living produces negative account. The coordinating conjunction "But" (l. 175) introduces the rhetorical question (epiplelxis), which turns the lines into an enthymeme. Thus Mercy reminds the audience that those who are idle will have difficulty justifying their actions on Judgment Day. To medieval men "ydullnes" meant more than it means today. "Ydullnes" meant not merely laziness or inaction but the practice of harmful or frivolous things in place of something useful (Coogan 50–51). The two enthymemes are joined together by the words "reson" (l. 173) and "acownte" (l. 177) because these two words are synonymous and mean "account" or "reckoning" (Conley 447): therefore, one must be accountable to God on Judgment Day for idle words and idle living.

The fact that the words reflect the man implies that worthy men will speak and behave in a moral fashion, whereas immoral men will utter empty rhetoric and lead a wasteful immoral life. Cicero again comes to mind since one of his major rhetorical doctrines is that "wisdom must accompany eloquence"; so does Quintilian, who emphasizes "moral purpose as well as rhetorical skill" (Murphy 98; 155). Whether influenced by these rhetoricians or not, the author of *Mankind* indicates that the "eloquence" of the villains lacks wisdom and moral foundation, a fact which surfaces in their idle lifestyles and will lead to damnation. Near the end of this judicial oration against idle words and idle living, Mercy strengthens his own position as a fair and moral man by refusing to criticize the latest fashion as such, blaming instead those who indulge in it improperly, and thus gaining more credibility and importance for his words: "The goode new gyse nowadays I wyll not dysalow. / I dyscomende þe vycyouse gyse" (ll. 182-83).

In addition to accountability for one's words and deeds Mercy informs Mankind that God will also test him during his lifetime (ll. 283-84) to determine his constancy. Mercy then draws an analogy between Job and Mankind (ll. 286-90). This technique of rhetorical amplification enhances the theme of the importance of language and ties it into the temptation of Mankind, which is a major aspect of the sovereignty theme:

> But he knows the way that I take; when he has
> tested me, I will come forth as gold.
>
> (Job 23:10)
>
> I have not departed from the commands of his lips;
> I have treasured the words of his mouth more than
> my daily bread.
>
> (Job 23:12)

Job knew that God tested him to make him a better man and that God's word was of paramount importance. The notion that Mankind's words are powerful and important to the future of his soul is thus connected through the allusion to Job and his tribulations to the all-powerful word of God. This reference to Job unites the themes of sovereignty and rhetoric with one image.

Although Mischief and his companions are the prime examples of empty rhetoric and the immoral way of living, Titivillus, which is the name given to Satan in this play, is the epitome of lies and the frivolous sinful life founded on evil. The choice of the name "Titivillus" is appropriate in the context of the rhetorical theme of the play. Titivillus is the name given to a demon who was forged from two separate demons. One of these demons is a dull devil who recorded misdeeds in church, such as talking during the service, and the other is a demon who carries a heavy sack filled with "syllables cut off, syncopated, or skipped over by clerics in reciting or chanting the psalms" (Jennings 8). Titivillus's literary development is greatest in medieval exempla attached to sermons and in didactic moral treatises (Jennings 8), although an evil spirit named Titivillus does appear in the Towneley *Judicum* (Jennings 51). Titivillus's literary tradition includes a large segment of fifteenth-century German and French drama, but the emphasis there is on his evil nature more than on his connection to misdeeds and idle language (Jennings 54). Regardless of whether the author or his audience knew of the European Titivillus, they would be familiar with the Titivillus of their sermons and moral treatises. The author reverses the role of Titivillus in *Mankind* and has him dispense idle language and horrid lies in an effort to pervert Mankind and win the game. Titivillus in *Mankind* is as certain of his ability with sophistic rhetoric as Mercy is of his "delectable" (1. 65) way of speaking. Moreover, Titivillus is arrogant when he makes his entrance in the second scene. Having no doubt that he can win Mankind's soul with his lies and insinuations, Titivillus boldly warns the audience not once but twice (1l. 476-77; 1l. 490-91) to beware of New Gyse and his companions because they are horse thieves. Since the horse symbolizes Mankind's soul, Titivillus warns the people in the audience to be on their guard against New Gyse and his cohorts and, by extension, against Titivillus as well because these rogues intend to steal Mankind's soul. This indirect warning illustrates total confidence to the point of arrogance since Titivillus believes that a warning is useless against the power of his tongue. This advance warning must be some sort of ethical code of devils, or, more likely, another aspect of the game.

When Titivillus enters the scene after the collection of money from the audience by New Gyse, Nowadays, and Nought, he declares in Latin that he is lord of all (1. 475), a position which puts him on God's level in this game. The author pushes the parallel between God and the Devil further by incorporating a test episode between Titivillus and the three derelicts who collected the money. By labeling the three rogues as horse thieves (1l. 476-77), Titivillus sets up the dramatic irony of the ensuing episode. The audience knows that Titivillus is the chief horse thief, and they know that he is aware of the money that the villains have collected from the audience. The test episode then increases the irony of the play as well as forming a structural link to the line in which Mercy tells Mankind that "God wyll proue yow son" (1. 283). Titivillus says, "Ego probo sic: [I test you thus] ser New Gyse, lende me a peny!" (1. 478). New Gyse responds:

> I haue a grett purse, ser, but I haue no monay.
> By þe masse, I fayll [lack] to farthyngys of an
>   halpeny;
> ȝyt hade I ten pound þis nyght þat was.
>   (1l. 479-81)

Titivillus then directs his question to Nowadays: "What is in þi purse? þou art a stout felow" (1. 482). Nowadays quickly answers:

> þe Deull haue the qwytt! I am a clen jentyllman.
> I prey Gode I be neuer wers storyde [less well
>   provided] than I am.
> Yt xall be otherwyse, I hope, or þis nyght passe.
> (11. 483-85)

Titivillus makes the same request of Nought: "Here now! I say þou hast many a peny" (1. 486). Nought replies:

> Non nobis, domine, non nobis [Not us, lord, not us],
>   by Sent Deny!
> þe Deull may daunce in my purse for ony peny;
> Yt ys as clen as a byrdys ars.
> (11. 487-89)

At this juncture Titivillus issues his second warning to the audience about the three villains and their tendency to steal horses, without commenting on what has just transpired. His point has been proved. As far as the test is concerned, the three rogues are indeed "constant" as Mercy says that Mankind must be. New Gyse, Nowadays, and Nought lie like the Devil's servants that they are. With each lying response the use of rhetorical devices increases, creating a kind of climactic order in the responses, an order which ends with Nought's very flowery rendition. New Gyse readily agrees that he has a large purse, but that purse is empty and he swears an oath, "By þe masse," (orcos) to that effect. Nowadays prefaces his answer with an exclamation expressing his outrage at the question (ecphonesis). Then he adds irony to the speech by declaring himself to be "a clen jentyllman"; neither "clen" nor a "jentyllman" is this disreputable fellow. Finally, Nowadays calls on God to keep him from being poorer than he is at the moment (deesis). Nought begins his lie with a phrase in Latin that also exhibits the figure epanalipsis with the repetition at the end of the clause of the initial words "non nobis" (Joseph 305). Even though this opening line outshines the other two lies by itself, Nought goes on to swear by a saint (orcos), quotes a proverb (paroemia) about the devil, and finishes with a simile comparing his purse to the cleanness of a "byrdys ars." The man has outdone himself. It is almost as if New Gyse, Nowadays, and Nought are competing in a liar's contest to see whose rhetoric could be the most florid while successfully evading the truth about their collecting gold coins before their master's arrival. The rogues passed the test in that by proving their mastery of lies and empty rhetoric, they have shown themselves worthy of their master and the damnation that he offers them. The episode illustrates another function of the collection scene in addition to representing the materialistic lifestyle. The greed for money prompts the three derelicts to display their deceit and fraud to the audience, a more effective method of exhibiting the evils of materialism than railing against it in a sermon that would likely fall on deaf ears anyway. The episode also allows the audience to see how well the Devil's servants can handle the language in order to serve their wicked purposes. The liveliness of the liar's contest will hold the people's attention and perhaps the message that they, too, can fall prey to such machinations will be absorbed.

Titivillus listens to the complaints of the three despicable ruffians about their injuries at the hands of Mankind and promises vengeance. When the three villains ask Titivillus to "speke to Mankynde" (l. 496) about his treatment of them, the use of the verb "speke" sets up the context of language rather than physical violence as a means of vengeance. Although "speke" could be used in an ironical sense, Nowadays's remark seems to strengthen the idea of a rhetorical meaning: "Remember my brokyn hede in þe worschyppe of þe fyve vowellys" (1. 497). Smart believes that a scribal error changed " 'v. volvellys' " from the manuscript into "v. wellys," which refers to the five wounds of Christ ("Some Notes on *Mankind*" 106); therefore, Nowadays's remarks refer to a variation of a charm referring to the five wounds of Christ. Nowadays uses this variation to remind Titivillus of his cries of pain when Mankind hit Nowadays and his friends with the shovel; however, the text does not list such cries as part of the dialogue. Nowadays simply says that he is "lyke neuer for to thryve [thrive], / I have such a buffett" (11. 382-83). It is thus possible that Nowadays expects Titivillus to wreak vengeance through words just as New Gyse has indicated with the verb "speke"; therefore, Nowadays is referring to persuasive use of language in an ironical way when he says "in þe worschyppe of þe fyve vowellys." If such is the case, no scribal error exists and the text stands. Titivillus does plan to use his rhetorical skill on Mankind after he sends the three whining fellows away: "To speke wyth Mankynde I wyll tary here þis tyde / And assay [try] hys goode purpose for to sett asyde" (11. 525-26). The verb "speke" echoes New Gyse's "speke," reinforcing the theory of language as the means to win the game and achieve vengeance simultaneously. The acknowledgment of Mankind's "good purpose" illustrates a recognition of Mankind's adherence to Mercy's doctrine and the advantage Mercy has in the game. Calling for quiet, Titivillus tells the audience his intention: "Qwyst! pesse! I xall go to hys ere and tytyll [whisper] þerin" (1. 557). The vehement call for silence indicates that Titivillus cannot tolerate any outside interference if his lies are to succeed. Not only does Titivillus require silence for his lies, but he must also remain unseen: "Euer I go invysybull, yt ys my jett [custom]" (1. 529). Mercy faces Mankind with the truth but Titivillus attacks him invisibly with lies. A few lines later Titivillus once again informs the audience of how he will win Mankind:

> I xall answere hym ad omnia quare [with a reason
>   for everything].
> Ther xall be sett abroche [opened up] a clerycall
>   [subtle] mater.
> I hope of [from] hys purpose to sett hym asyde.
>   (11. 578-80)

The Latin phrase indicates that Titivillus will have an answer for all of Mankind's questions. Titivillus plans to "whisper" lies into Mankind's ear to answer his questions and to lure him from Mercy's side. Line 580 repeats the idea of setting Mankind aside from his purpose in almost the same words Titivillus uses earlier in this line: "Ande assay [try] hys goode purpose for to sett asyde" (1. 526). This repetition of the same idea in different words, which is similar to the figure commoratio, emphasizes Titivillus's determination to win and links the two speeches.

    Titivillus proceeds to put into practice what he has arrogantly informed the audience that he would do and whispers into Mankind's ear, planting the idea that he must stop his prayers and relieve himself at once:

> Qwyst! pesse! I xall go to hys ere and tytyll þerin.
> A schorte preyere thyrlyth hewyn [pierce heaven]:
>   of þi preyere blyn [cease].
> þou art holyer þen euer was ony of þi kyn.
> Aryse and avent [relieve] þe! Nature compellys.
>   (11. 557-59)

The first whisper deals with a feigned call of nature too urgent to ignore and serves indirectly to pull Mankind away from his prayers. Before the "whispering" began Titivillus had already deceived Mankind by placing a board in the ground to make Mankind's digging very difficult and by mixing weeds with the corn to ruin it and cause Mankind to throw down his shovel in disgust, thereby parting himself from honest work symbolized by the shovel (11. 532–49). The honest labor is Mankind's first line of defense against the Devil and Titivillus picks up the shovel and carries it out of Mankind's reach to insure against a change of heart. The prayer service symbolizes Mankind's remaining faith in God and is his second line of defense. Now that both honest labor and religious faith are gone, Titivillus uses his second whisper as a direct attack in the form of an absurd lie about Mercy:

> Qwyst! pesse! þe Deull ys dede! I xall goo ronde
> [whisper] in hys ere.
> Alasse, Mankynde, alasse! Mercy stown [has
> stolen] a mere [mare]!
> He ys runn away fro hys master, þer wot [knows]
> no man where;
> Moreouer, he stale both a hors and a nete [cow].
> (11. 593–96)

This second whisper opens exactly as the first with a plea for silence, and the intention to whisper in Mankind's ear is presented in similar words, rhetorically linking the two passages. The diacope in which *Mankynde* separates the repetitions of "alasse" marks the beginning of Mankind's slide into the lifestyle of the rogues. The choice of a horse as the object of Mercy's thieving joins this speech to Titivillus's first speech accusing the three villains of being horse thieves. The horse symbolizes Mankind's soul as one aspect of the sovereignty theme in this play; therefore, the irony of this episode with Titivillus is heightened when Mercy is accused of being a horse thief. Mankind was trying voluntarily to be a follower of Mercy's teachings. Titivillus and his followers are the real horse thieves, who are attempting to swipe Mankind's soul with lies and deceit. The rhetoric theme thus intertwines at this point with the horse image and, by extension, the body-soul image.

The lie about Mercy grows by leaps and bounds in much the same way as the lies of New Gyse, Nowadays, and Nought grew in the liars' contest. At first Mercy is accused of stealing "a mere" (1. 594). By line 596 Mercy has stolen "both a hors and a nete [cow]." From there the lie continues to grow:

> But ȝet I herde sey he brake hys neke as he rode in
> Fraunce;
> But I thynke he rydyth on þe galouse, to lern for to
> daunce.
> Bycause of hys theft, þat ys hys gouernance
> [conduct].
>
> (11. 597–99)

The reference to dancing connects to the episode in the first scene in which New Gyse and his cohorts try to get Mercy to dance to their tune (11. 85–97), to the line by Titivillus (1. 528) in which he promises to make Mankind "Dawance anoþer trace," and, indirectly, to the episode of the near-hanging suffered by New Gyse (11. 615–20) following Titivillus's departure. Although the rogues are unable to make Mercy dance to their tune, now Titivillus has Mercy learning to dance at the end of a rope in this life. The irony occurs because it is Titivillus's own man, New Gyse, who actually does this dance. The implication is that death results from a failure to dance to Titivillus's tune; however, the opposite is true, a fact which increases the dramatic irony. Titivillus incorporates yet another facet of the horse metaphor into this lie in the lines describing

Mercy's ride on the gallows (1. 598). The two forms of the word "ride" ("rode"; "rydyth") constitute the figure polyptoton, which is the use of various forms of the same word (Joseph 306). This figure sets up the metaphor comparing horseback riding and hanging through the use of antistasis in which the same word is used in two different senses. Line 597 refers to riding a real horse in France, whereas line 598's "rydyth on þe galouse" refers to the gallows as a metaphorical horse. The next line points out that hanging is the result of the crime of theft. If one accepts the horse as a symbol of Mankind's soul, the theft of it from Mercy by Titivillus does result in death—Mankind's eternal death. This lie contains a grain of truth.

Titivillus continues to embellish the lie as he warns Mankind against Mercy:

> Trust no more on hym, he ys a marryde [ruined] man.
> Mekyll [great] sorow with þi spade beforn [earlier] þou hast wrought.
> Aryse and aske mercy of Neu Gyse, Nowadays, and Nought.
> þei cun avyse þe for þe best; lett þer goode wyll be sought;
> Ande þi own wyff brethell [deceive], and take þe a lemman [mistress].
> (11. 600-04)

Saving the largest part of his lie for the end, Titivillus encourages Mankind not to trust Mercy, but to seek forgiveness and good counsel from the three villains. The sovereignty theme gains a foothold here with the mention of adultery. Such an action could ostensibly make a wife understand who was master, as well as making it clear to God what sort of life Mankind now leads. The reference connects to the imagery of domestic sovereignty in the first scene, linking the two parts of the play together.

Two references to the "neke-verse" occur before and after this episode in which Titivillus uses sophistic rhetoric to win Mankind to his side in the game, thereby forming a kind of rhetorical frame. During the Middle Ages, one could avoid being hanged if he could recite or read from the Bible, usually Psalm 50:3, a Latin verse. New Gyse mentions this alternative immediately before Titivillus begins his whispering campaign: "If we may be take, we com no more hethyr. / Lett ws con [learn] well owr neke-verse, þat we haue not a cheke [disaster]" (11. 519–20). Twelve lines after Titivillus's departure, New Gyse describes his near-hanging and points out that Mischief escaped because he knew his Bible verse: "Myscheff ys a convicte, for he coude [knew] hys neke-verse" (1. 619). This emphasis on the reading or reciting of a Bible verse to save one's life underscores the theme of the importance of language, since words in this case can actually prevent death. On the symbolic level, if one knows the Bible, the repository of Mercy's doctrine, then one can save his soul and avoid eternal death.

Mankind, the symbolic ball in this diabolical game, has great difficulty in recognizing the idle language and sophistic rhetoric of his new acquaintances; however, he does not have the ability to appreciate Mercy's gift with language: "O, yowr louely wordys to my soull are swetere þen hony" (1. 225). Mankind's faith may not be as strong as it should be, which contributes to his inability to see through Titivillus's lies. When Mankind responds to Mercy's blessing, he employs epanalepsis by repeating the word "amen" at the beginning and at the end of his exclamation: "Amen, for sent charyte, amen!" (1. 310). The use of this figure of repetition effectively sets up the notion borne out by the next four lines that Mankind "doth protest too much":

> Now blyssyde be Jhesu! My soull ys well sacyatt
> Wyth þe mellyfluouse doctryne of þis worschyppfull
> > man.
> The rebellyn of my flesch now yt ys superatt;
> Thankynge be Gode of þe commynge þat I kam.
>
> (11. 311–14)

Juxtaposed to the emphatic "amens" and the invocation to St. Charity is the device called eulogia in which Mankind pronounces a blessing on Jesus (Joseph 393), declaring that his soul is satisfied and that the rebellion of the flesh is conquered. Mankind labels Mercy's teaching as "þe mellyfluouse doctryne," which indicates a recognition of the way Mercy uses language to instruct Mankind. The word "mellyfluouse" connects to Mankind's metaphorical comparison of Mercy's rhetorical technique to the smooth rich flow of honey (1. 225). This reference establishes another structural link in addition to furthering the theme of the importance of how one uses language. The last of these four lines incorporates polyptoton in which words of the same root are repeated in different forms (Joseph 306): "commynge" and "kam" (*cam*). The line seems to be an indirect form of eulogia in blessing God that Mankind was born. The polyptoton emphasizes the point. Mankind uses several emphatic rhetorical devices in these five lines (11. 310–14), giving the segment an overly enthusiastic tone, which indicates that Mankind may be overcompensating for something. Since the rest of the speech is devoted to a method of defense from superstitious charms, the "something" might be weak faith:

> Her wyll I sytt and tytll in þis papyr
> The incomparable astat of my promycyon.
> Worschypfull sourence, I haue wretyn here
> The gloryuse remembrance of my nobyll condycyon

To haue remos and memory of mysylff þus wretyn
   yt ys,
To defende me from all superstycyus charmys.
                                          (ll. 315-20)

Again the playwright focuses the attention on words, the written word in this case, as a protection from harm. Mankind writes what he terms as the "remembrance" of his "nobyll condycyon." If "nobyll condycyon" can be interpreted as Mankind's position as a child of God, who is the ruler of the universe, then Mankind is attempting to make his situation concrete and visible to all by writing it down and using it as a lucky charm similar to a rabbit's foot. The apostrophe to the audience, "Worschypfull souerence," brings the people into the action and implies that both Mankind and the audience may have weak faith, requiring the additional trappings of superstition to feel safe. The Latin phrase that Mankind writes is from Job 24:15 and translates: "Remember, man, that you are dust and unto dust you will return" (l. 321). This phrase echoes Mankind's first line in the play, tying the two speeches together and underscoring the notion that God created him and holds great power over him. The line "Lo, I ber on my bryst þe bagge of myn armys" (322) picks up the motif of "Crystys own knight" (l. 228) and emphasizes the idea that weak faith, a failing of the Arthurian knights, might also be a failing of Mankind's. Although W. K. Smart believes that the badge is a sign of the cross that Mankind hangs around his neck (Eccles 320nM322), the text does not support that theory, indicating instead that Mankind writes the Bible verse on the piece of paper that he hangs about his neck.

Mankind may be easily duped by sophistic rhetoric as a result of a weakness in his belief, but his intentions are good, and he wishes to work hard to avoid idleness:

> I her a felow speke; wyth hym I wyll not mell.
> Thys erth wyth my spade I xall assay [try] to
>   delffe [dig]
> To eschew ydullness I do yt myn own selfe.
> I prey Gode send yt hys fusyon [plenty]!
>   (11. 327–30)

In spite of his good intentions, Mankind uses the personal pronoun "I" five times within four lines, indicating that Mankind takes pride in himself and his achievements. The last line (330) echoes the wording and structure of New Gyse's plea, "God sende ws goode ferys!" (1. 323), illustrating that Mankind's language may not be backed up as strongly by feeling as it should be and that he is becoming more like New Gyse than he realizes. Mercy warns Mankind that God will test his constancy to determine his worthiness for heaven (11. 283–84). This warning concerning the test actually initiates Mankind's indulgence in the sin of pride. Mankind misunderstands his encounter with New Gyse, Nowadays, and Nought, believing that God sent them in order to allow Mankind to overpower them and be a hero:

> Now I thanke Gode, knelynge on my kne.
> Blyssyde be hys name! he ys of hye degre.
> By the subsyde of hys grace þat he hath sente me
> Thre of myn enmys I have putt to flight.
>   (11. 392–95)

After misconstruing this event, Mankind slips briefly into pride again:

> I promytt yow þes felouse wyll no more cum here,
> For summe of þem, certenly, were summewhat to

nere.
My fadyr Mercy avysyde me to be of a goode chere
And agayn my enemys manly for to fight.
I xall convycte þem, I hope, euerychon.
(ll. 401-05)

These words have a boastful tone. Mankind believes himself to be so menacing that the three useless fellows dare not return. The reference to Mercy's advice to "resyst lyke a man" (l. 224), serves as a structural link as well as reiterating the idea that Mankind is subject to human frailty and can resist to the best of his ability within the limitations of his humanity. The prominence of the pronoun "I" in these lines coupled with the feeling of power exhibited by his "promytt" that the rogues will not return support this theory of Mankind's indulgence in the worst of human frailties— pride. Mankind does, however, soon remember that God is the source of his power, and he tries to make amends for his lapse:

ȝet I say amysse, I do yt not alon.
Wyth þe helpe of þe grace of Gode I resyst my fon
Ande þer malycyuse herte.
(ll. 406-08)

Mankind addresses the audience, telling them that he is going to get his corn to plant and asking their indulgence until his return:

Wyth my spade I wyll departe, my worschyppull
    souerence
And lyue euer wyth labure to corecte my insolence.

I xall go fett corn for my londe; I prey yow of
    pacyence;

> Ryght son I xall reverte.
>
> (ll. 409-12)

The apostrophe pulls the audience into the action at the point where the people need to be identified with Mankind's behavior. The reference to the seed corn recalls the corn proverb that ends Mercy's opening speech, which frames the action of the play, thus linking the two together and aiding in the cohesion of the play. The scene thus ends by recalling the corn metaphor and with Mankind's exit with his spade, the symbol of his honest labor, good deeds, and, for the moment, the symbol of his victory over New Gyse, Nowadays, and Nought. He still exhibits a great deal of confidence with seven personal pronouns ("I") in the last speech (ll. 401-11), despite his language to the contrary. Carrying the spade into the second scene with him, Mankind provides a visual as well as a symbolic link between the two parts.

Mankind balks at having to ask for mercy again, saying that he is unworthy; however, the words that he chooses seem to indicate a vestige of pride remaining and a disinclination to expose his transgressions:

> What, aske mercy ȝet onys agayn?
> Alas, yt were a wyle [craft] petycyun.
> Ewry to offend and euer to aske mercy, yt ys a
>   puerilite [childish thing].
> Yt ys so abhominabyll to rehers my iterat [repeated]
>   transgrescion,
> I am not worthy to hawe mercy be no possibilite.
>
> (ll. 819-22)

Continuing to ask for mercy is childish for whom? Mankind does not make that clear. Reciting his repeated transgressions is abominable for whom? His initial reaction— "What, aske mercy ʒet onys again?"—sets the tone for the speech. Mankind is thinking out loud about the things he will have to do to regain mercy, and he realizes that he will have to humble himself and apologize. Mankind is not sure that he wants to do this. Remnants of pride still linger. However, one cannot acknowledge a reluctance to practice humility; therefore, Mankind tries another strategy to avoid the issue by pointing out his unworthiness instead. Mercy, realizing that Mankind is engaging in the empty rhetoric that Mercy disdains and despises, prays to Jesus to put Mankind back on the right track:

> O Mankend, my singler [special] solas, þis is a
> lamentabyll excuse.
> The dolorus [anguished] terys of my hert, how þei
> begyn to amownt!
> O pirssid Jhesu, help þou þis synfull synner to
> redouce [back to the right way]!
> Nam hec est mutacio dextre Excelsi; ertit impios et
> non sunt. [Now this is the movement of the
> right hand of the Most High; He turns the
> impious and they are no more.]
> (11. 823-26)

Mercy incorporates an apostrophe to Mankind and an apostrophe to Jesus along with vehement supplication (deesis) to underscore his emotion and his feeling of urgency at Mankind's obstinacy. The use of deesis serves as a point of departure for the Latin prayer (paradigesis), which illustrates what God does to those who fail to return to the right path and serve Him as their Sovereign Lord. After this prayer, Mercy applies the wisdom of the words to Mankind's own situation, using the same verbal structure that

Titivillus uses when he has possession of Mankind:

> Aryse and aske mercy, Mankend, and be associat
> to me.
> (1. 827)
> Aryse and aske mercy of Neu Gyse, Nowadays and
> Nought.
> (1. 602)

Similar words and sentence structure indicate the parallel in the situations, except that Mercy now has the winning edge in the game. Mankind pushes on in his prideful way, saying that he does not believe God's "egall justyse" (1. 831) will allow a wretch as sinful as he is to be restored, but Mercy quotes the Bible to soothe him; however, Mankind remains obstinate to Mercy's pleas and responds by punning on Mercy's name:

> þan mercy, good Mercy! What ys a man wythowte
> mercy?
> Lytyll ys our parte of paradyse were mercy ne were.
> Good Mercy, excuse the ineuytabyll objeccion of my
> gostly enmy.
> (11. 835–37)

The pun is actually a form of diaphora in which the common noun is repeated in both the sense of a name and of a quality in this case (Joseph 306). This flippant attitude toward Mercy indicates that Mankind still is not ready to yield sovereignty to God. The mention of "gostly enmy" indicates the lingering influence of the Devil, which compounds the problem. Attempting to deal with this lingering influence, Mercy uses a metaphorical comparison between the devil's hold on Mankind and a wound curable by surgery:

If ȝe fele ȝoursylfe trapped in þe snare of your gostly
    enmy,
Aske mercy anon; be ware of þe contynuance.
Whyll a wond ys fresch yt ys prowyd curabyll be
    surgery,
þat yf yt procede ouyrlong, yt ys cawse of gret
    grewans.
                                            (ll. 855-58)

When Mankind says to Mercy, "ȝe are worthy to have my love" (l. 872), it is apparent that Mankind did not really think himself unworthy of mercy but the other way around, a most arrogant display of pride. Mankind finally overcomes his pride, effects a change in attitude, and admits his sins: "A, yt swemyth [grieves] my hert to thynk how onwysely [foolishly] I haue wroght" (l. 875). His experiences with Titivillus and his followers will help him in his ability to recognize false rhetoric and make him stronger in the next round of the game.

The playwright creatively employs the scatological humor in *Mankind*, which so grievously offended many scholars, to illustrate graphically the state of the souls of those who engage in idle language and idle living. This symbolism is established in the last two lines of Mercy's horse proverb, which can be extended to include the body-soul dichotomy in the context of sovereignty theme:

Yf he be fede ouerwell he wyll dysobey
Ande in happe cast his master in þe myre.
                                            (ll. 243-44)

The ideal situation features the wisdom of the soul in command of the desires of the body; however, overindulgence in the material and sensual things of the world will cause the body to throw off the wisdom of the soul. The image of the soul as the master lying in the "myre" graphically illustrates the dirt and filth that attaches itself to the soul when the flesh gains the upper hand in their battle for supremacy, a motif that is reflected in all of the instances of scatological humor in this serious play. This sort of humor is indulged in by those characters—Mischief, New Gyse, Nowadays, and Nought—whose souls are besmirched by the filth of sin. The scatological humor depicts the frailty of human nature as well as the mark of sin. The tendency to be idle, to have fun, to lie, if necessary, is basic human nature unless otherwise disciplined. Titivillus links lies with this sort of humor when he compares lies metaphorically to excrement: "I have sent hym forth to schyte [void as excrement] lesynges [lies]" (1. 568). Scatological humor, therefore, becomes another aspect of the rhetorical theme, giving it a broader range. Titivillus, pleased with his power to force Mankind to put the needs of his body above those of his soul, engages in the rhetorical device called paradiegesis (Taylor 154) in which the fact that Mankind left vespers is used to prove the point that Titivillus is very wise:

> Mankynde was besy in hys prayers, ȝet I dyde
> [caused] hym aryse
> He ys conveyde, be Cryst, from hys dyvyn seruyce.
>
> Whethere ys he, trow [think] ȝe? Iwysse [certainly]
> I am wonder wyse.
> (11. 565–67)

To add validity to his proof Titivillus swears (orcos) by his opponent in the game, Christ, whose connection with truth is irrefutable. By metaphorically connecting Mankind's actions to a basic bodily function (1. 568), Titivillus vividly ties the scatological humor to the contamination of Mankind's soul. As a result line 566 has also been "conveyde [taken]" from Christ's "devyn servyce." The metaphor merely illustrates the fact that the soul as well as the body has left Christ's service. The "call of Nature" is actually the call of the Devil. Titivillus juxtaposes an exemplum which illustrates his powers of illusion next to these lines, metaphorically connecting the bodily functions with the status of the soul:

> Yff ȝe haue ony syluer, in happe pure brasse,
> Take a lytyll powder of Parysch and cast ouer hys
>   face,
> Ande ewyn [exactly] in þe howll-flyght [twilight] let
>   hym passe.
> Titivillus kan lerne yow many praty [clever]
>   thyngys.
>
>   (11. 569-72)

By informing the audience how one can use powder of Paris to make brass pass for silver, Titivillus displays his ability at subterfuge, while simultaneously creating within the members of the audience the illusion that they are sharing in the secrets of the Devil. The exemplum serves several symbolic functions in the speech. First, it illustrates Titivillus's chief role as a perpetrator of illusion. Second, the story should warn the audience that subterfuge can make a thing appear more valuable than it is, and that one cannot always believe his eyes. Third, the juxtaposition with the humorous passages creates a subtle connection between illusion and scatology, which indicates that illusion can also be a sign of a tainted soul. The exemplum closes with the implicit invitation to join Titivillus and his companions in order to learn clever things.

    At the end of the second scene Mischief has a filthy accident and soils himself: "A myscheff go wyth [the devil take it]! here I haue a foull fall [filthy accident]. / Hens awey fro me, or I xall beschyte

116   A Diabolical Game to Win Man's Soul

[soil] yow all" (11. 730–31). Coming at the end of the second scene in which Mankind has defected to the side of Evil, the picturesque rendition of a human being soiled by his own excrement and his warning to others to keep their distance or risk contamination takes on symbolic meaning. The audience is being warned forcefully that the filth of sin is inherently present in Mankind and without God's mercy we cannot help but contaminate our own souls and those who come in contact with us. Irony abounds in this episode, since Mankind has symbolically stained himself with his own sinful nature in the second scene by getting too close to Mischief, New Gyse, Nowadays, and Nought. Mischief's accident is a concrete rendering of the symbolic action in the second scene. A similar situation occurs in the third scene when Nought befouls himself with an accident on his foot:

> I am doynge of my nedynges; be ware how ȝe schott!
> Fy, fy, fy! I haue fowll arayde my fote.
> Be wyse for a schotynge wyth yowr takyllys, for
>   Gode wott
> My fote ys fowly ouerschett [covered with dung].
>   (11. 783–86)

Nought warns others to be careful, but, of course, they, too, are contaminated as badly as Nought, whose accident is the visual representation of the sins of them all. In addition to these examples, other instances of this type of humor are sprinkled in strategic places throughout the play, such as the filthy rhyme that Nowadays wants Mercy to translate into Latin, which effects another tie between the scatological humor and practitioners of empty, scurrilous rhetoric (11. 131–134); the Christmas song, which blasphemously ridicules the Mass (11. 335–43); Nought's advice to Mankind to become self-sufficient agriculturally, which supports the sovereignty theme; and Mankind's reference to his flesh as that "stynkyng dungehyll" (1. 204), which connects to the allusion to Job, thus yielding a precedent for scatology as a concrete representation of Mankind's corrupt nature. The study of Job was the focus of a long commentary by Gregory the Great (540?–604) entitled *In expositionem Beati Job Moralia*. This commentary pointed out that Job sat on a dunghill by his own choice in order to remind himself of Man's origin and of the corruption of Man's flesh (Neuss 47–48). This connection adds still another dimension to the Job allusion. In another theological treatise, *De vitis patrum*, there is a reference to demons who appeared to monks as pigs and spread excrement amidst the monks when they talked of secular things. When the monks returned to edifying topics of conversation, they "would have to be cleansed by attendant heavenly spirits" (Jennings 4). Given the levels of meaning involved in the scatological humor, it is possible that the author of *Mankind* knew one or both of these treatises. If not, then his skillful incorporation of the scatological humor into the play to fulfill symbolic, thematic, and structural needs is further evidence of his high degree of sophistication and artistic ability. The symbolism and layers of meaning inherent in this humor would not be too complex even for a rural audience, because people in the Middle Ages were visually oriented as a result of the Priests' use of visual association as a means of educating the illiterate congregations. These people knew and understood symbolism and allegory (Pollack 56).

    A rhetorical analysis of *Mankind* thus reveals that the playwright uses numerous figures of repetition, grammatical schemes of construction, figures of substitution, figures of amplification, figures of emotional appeal, figures of allusion, metaphors, puns, techniques of argument, and even a few vices of language in his efforts to support the themes and the structure of his play.

Without the distraction of artistic interpretations by the actors in a dramatic performance, one can see that the play itself is a work of literary art. The playwright skillfully employs his rhetorical expertise to present the familiar morality play conflict between the forces of Good and Evil and the well-known religious doctrines inherent in that struggle in a creatively different way, carefully incorporating all elements into its structural and thematic texture. The playwright builds the dramatic action of *Mankind* on the metaphor of the game and uses the popular medieval framework device to enclose the action with Mercy's words of wisdom. The game is played with words and the object of the game is the soul of Mankind; therefore, the two major themes of *Mankind* are sovereignty and rhetoric, with other thematic motifs denoting Christian ideals weaving in and out of the play. The scatological humor is important thematically and structurally to *Mankind* and has not been used solely in an effort to appeal to a rural audience.

Evidence in favor of the underlying game metaphor resides primarily in the language and structure of the play with additional support from the medieval literary tradition of sinister comedy depicted by MacAlindon in which the diabolical game plays an important role. The words "game," "play," and "sport" are used many times in the play in connection with the proceedings at hand. Mischief specifically sets up the game metaphor when he tells Mercy that he has come "to make yow game" (1. 69). After corrupting Mankind and bringing him over to the Devil's side, Titivillus remarks, "for I have don my game" (1. 605). Two references to game-playing equipment further enhance the metaphor—the football and the net. After Mankind has gone from Mercy's side to Mischief's, New Gyse rather irrelevantly asks the innkeeper for a football. Symbolically, the rogues already have a football in the form of Mankind, who is now in their possession, but whom Mercy intends to get back. The net image is introduced when Mercy warns

A Rhetorical Analysis of *Mankind* – Part II 119

Mankind that Titivillus will hang a net in front of his eyes to deceive him. Not only does this image symbolize the empty rhetoric of lies and deceit and create a structural link with its reiteration by Titivillus in the second scene and Mankind in the third, but the net image with its connotations of a blindfold for the eyes has an indirect connection to the children's game of Blind Man's Bluff, which dates back to the Roman Empire, yielding yet another facet of the game metaphor. The structure of the action further strengthens the notion of the game metaphor in that the opposing sides seem to take turns; there is the additional indication that this situation is only the first round and that the game will continue until Mankind's death symbolically signals the end of the contest. The two opposing sides are, of course, God and the Devil, who is Titivillus in this play. As the ultimate forces of Good and Evil, God and Titivillus are not supposed to participate personally, but are represented on earth by Mercy, who aligns himself with God in his opening speech, a position which is underscored throughout the play by various rhetorical techniques enhancing Mercy's ethos, and by Mischief, who aligns himself with the Devil when he refuses to obey Mercy's command to leave because Mercy did not ask it in the Devil's name, and with other rhetorical devices in the play. The two men are worthy adversaries, although Mercy has the upper hand rhetorically because he has truth and wisdom to support his eloquence. Mercy completely overwhelms Mischief with the elevated language and superb rhetorical technique of his opening speech; therefore, Mischief decides that the best strategy in this game is to use mockery and derision to undermine Mercy's carefully constructed ethos and cause his arguments to seem invalid. New Gyse, Nowadays, and Nought quickly follow this plan and mock Mercy's speech patterns, his imagery, his Latin quotations, and his serious tone at every encounter. Since Mischief's mocking strategy is insufficient to overpower Mercy, Mischief obeys Mercy and leaves, giving Mercy the first turn at persuading Mankind to allow God to have sovereignty over his life. Once Mercy instructs Mankind in the proper Christian behavior and warns him against idle living, idle language, and Titivillus, Mercy leaves Mankind to the opposition. New Gyse, Nowadays, and Nought get the first turn, but are unsuccessful at luring Mankind into a frivolous life and away from his honest work. a recurring thematic motif symbolized by the spade. Mercy is still in possession of the ball. Mischief panics, saying that he was there at the "begynnynge of þe game and arguyde wyth Mercy" (1. 417), implying that he should have been able to do something then to prevent losing Mankind. The rogues apparently decide that cheating is the only way, and Titivillus enters to corrupt Mankind personally. When Mercy learns of this situation, he vows to regain Mankind, which frightens the villains, who realize that Mercy's rhetorical ability is superior to theirs and that he will regain the ball (Mankind). To forestall this situation New Gyse decides to get Mankind to commit suicide while he is still in their possession, and then they will win the entire game not just another round; however, Mercy comes into the scene and, with difficulty, overcomes Mankind's pride and convinces him once more to give sovereignty over his life to God, not to Titivillus. Mercy sends Mankind on his way with a warning speech that he must not sin again and that he must beware of Titivillus with his net. Mankind must also control the sensual nature of his body. The implication of these lines is that Mankind has learned from his experiences but that Evil is still an ever-present danger to which human beings are subject until they die. The game goes on, even though the play ends.

The literary tradition of sinister comedy that MacAlindon describes revolves around the idea of the abominable game and allows the mixture of comic scenes with serious scenes in religious works to enhance the moral message of the serious parts of the work. The comic scenes are marked with mockery and irony and the villains are witty, intelligent, deceptive, and powerful. *Mankind's* comic scenes sharpen Mercy's moral lessons by depicting graphically the idle lifestyle and the idle language of practitioners of such frivolous existences. The rogues are not admirable; they are despicable. Their foul language depicts the foul state of their souls, a fact recorded in the Bible and with which the medieval audience would be familiar. The two characters who actually befoul themselves with excrement are exhibiting the dirt on their souls and are illustrating to the audience that human nature is such that one can contaminate his own soul without outside influence, if he does not control his sinful nature and yield sovereignty to God. Titivillus is the epitome of the witty, intelligent, and deceitful villain described by MacAlindon. Titivillus puts himself on God's level when he enters, saying in Latin that he is "lord of lords." His power and intelligence are apparent in his "testing" of the three villains and in his corruption of Mankind. Mischief handles himself well rhetorically, as do Nowadays, Nought, and New Gyse, but they are inferior in intelligence and demeanor to Titivillus. All of the comic scenes are laced with irony and mockery, since derision is the villains's method of proceeding in the game. *Mankind* thus exhibits the characteristics found in other works in this tradition. The author mixes the comic and the serious to support his themes on a secondary level, using the intelligent, mocking, and deceitful Titivillus and his bumbling cohorts to display the threat to Mankind's soul from several directions simultaneously.

Mercy depends on his strong ethos and rhetorical expertise to win the game. Mercy's nearness to God and his genuine concern for the welfare of Mankind and, by extension through the judicious use of apostrophes, of the audience as well, are the major elements of his character, which permeate the framework speeches and filter through the action itself. In addition to establishing the strong ethos for Mercy, the opening speech in the frame sets up the themes and motifs that weave through the play underscoring the author's message and providing structural coherence. The first stanza establishes the adversaries in the game by contrasting the subject of the lines, God, with the hissing [s] sound representing the Devil, who is later referred to as "gostly enmy," "mortall enmye," and "venymousse serpente" (1. 27; 1. 40). This stanza introduces the sovereignty theme with the emphasis on our need to be obedient servants to God, who is Creator and Lord of all. Christ's sacrifice is mentioned and then captured as a thematic motif in the "dere bought" oath that echoes throughout the play. A common Biblical simile comparing Christ to a lamb is used in the frame and connects through the water imagery of the frame to similar imagery in the action when Mercy is labeled the "well" of virtue, further enhancing Mercy's ethos and supporting the sovereignty theme with a connection to Christ's sacrifice. The author cleverly gains several nuances of meaning by the use of a common rhetorical figure. The "dere bought" oath is put into the mouths of Mischief and New Gyse to dramatize their barren souls and to create an ironic atmosphere through the use of Mercy's favorite oath by those who have no claim to it. Such a technique will draw attention to Christ's great sacrifice for all mankind in a way a more familiar approach cannot do. Other Christian virtues which appear in the frame and become recurring thematic motifs are the need to perform good deeds and honest work, to avoid idleness, and to disregard the material things in life. The necessity of being accountable for one's behavior at Judgment Day is part of the instruction of the opening speech. Mercy uses a famous Biblical proverb at the end of his initial speech, which sums up in a vivid way the essence of his message. The proverb is the corn proverb which says that the corn is saved and the chaff is burned. All of Mercy's advice leads here, because if Mankind lives up to the

Christian virtues displayed in the opening speech, he will have yielded sovereignty to God, which is the thrust of the message. This corn metaphor is imitated in a sarcastic and mocking fashion by Mischief and by New Gyse and his friends at various points in the action, providing a structural link for the first two scenes and supporting the sovereignty theme in a negative way through the consequences of failure to allow God control and to yield to the Devil instead. The "reap what you sow" proverb illustrates another facet of the grain metaphor, supporting the sovereignty theme from the angle of the consequences of one's deeds and words. Although sovereignty over Mankind's soul is the object of the diabolical game, the emphasis, naturally, is on God's sovereignty as the only real choice. The thematic threads instituted in the initial speech are tied off in Mercy's speech after Mankind's exit. The notion that allowing God sovereignty over Mankind's life protects him from the "vemynousse serpente" in the initial speech connects to protection from "wyckyd captivite" in the final lines (905). A reference to Christ's love of all mankind as the reason God's son became human (1. 907) ties into the idea of Christ's sacrifice in the first speech and in the "dere bought" oath. The need to disregard the material things is summed up in the contention that the world is a "vanity" (1. 909). God's help is invoked to aid Mankind in his battle to keep his sensual nature in check. Accountability is reiterated with the warning of "dew examinacion" (1. 908). Mercy calls on God to be merciful to the audience which is a form of optatio and connects to the same optatio in the opening speech. The various thematic threads are thus neatly bound up by the playwright at the end of the play.

Although the second major theme, the importance of language and its usage, is not specifically mentioned in the framework as the sovereignty theme and the Christian ideals that depict the various aspects of that theme are mentioned, the elevated vocabulary and

124 A Diabolical Game to Win Man's Soul

the rhetorical virtuosity displayed in the playwright's use of commoratio, optatio, anaphora, antimetabole, and alliteration indirectly underscore the theme of rhetoric. Not only does Mercy's speech begin the framework of the play, but the hissing [s] sound representing the Devil frames Mercy's advice with 21 [s] sounds in the first and last stanzas of that speech. Rhetoric as such is specifically referred to when Mercy chastises Mischief for interrupting his "talking delectable" (1. 65). The notion that words are the method of proceeding in the game gains credence from Mischief's remark that he "arguyde" with Mercy at the beginning of the game (11. 417-18). The three disreputable characters ask Titivillus to "speke" to Mankind about his injuring them. Titivillus says that he will "speke" to Mankind in order to distract him from his good intentions (1. 496; 1. 525). The Devil then becomes invisible and, as a picture of unseen Evil, he "whispers" his lies into Mankind's ear. At several points in the play, Mercy speaks of idle language and the fact that the rogues will be accountable for every word they utter. Mercy's wonderful judicial oration condemning New Gyse, Nowadays, and Nought as "worse then beasts" and berating idle language and idle living effectively convicts the villains as practitioners of empty rhetoric and empty lifestyles (11. 161-85). Mercy also compliments the rhetoric of the villains with "Few words, few and well sett" (1. 102). The culprits tie language into the new fashion with "Many words and shortly sett," thereby adding another layer of meaning to the theme (1. 104). An emphasis on the written word appears with Nought's recording of the mock manor court's ,proceedings. Stress is placed on how the writing looks not on what it says. In line 692 Nought is compared to "Tulli," who scholars agree is Cicero. This comparison effectively strengthens the notion of a strong rhetorical theme, especially in light of Mercy's stress on the wisdom behind eloquence. Mercy also says moral purpose if important in language, which is

Quintilian's point, but no mention is made of this rhetorician. Two instances appear in the play in which words have the power to protect Mankind from harm. The first is the written verse that Mankind hangs around his neck to ward off superstitious charms and the second is the "neck verse" to which the villains refer, which is a Latin Bible verse that a person could either read or recite to save himself from hanging. This is a subtle way of reinforcing the idea that words are powerful and Mankind must be careful of his language. The use of the name "Titivillus" for the Devil bolsters the rhetorical theme, since that name is associated in literary tradition with idle language and misdeeds. The reference to Job subtly lends support to the importance of words in that Job said that he valued God's words more than life itself, which also forms a tenuous connection between the words of the play and God's word, again underscoring the power of the word in general and God's word in particular. Kathleen Ashley has already pointed out that the play makes a strong distinction between God's word and words of the Devil and of the world (129). The liars' contest among New Gyse, Nowadays, and Nought, which is set up by the collection scene, is a prime example of their empty rhetoric and a creative way to warn the audience of the deceitful language of such people. Mankind receives a new jacket fashioned from his long robe after his "initiation" into the ranks of Mischief and his comrades. Symbolizing the new fashion, this jacket connotes the new fashion in language, as well. Mankind's new allies abuse the new way of speaking, turning it into sophism and lies. A possibility exists that the jacket could have been a result of the influence of *Piers Plowman*, which scholars believe has influenced other aspects of the play. Haukyn's jacket stained with sin depicts the state of his soul, and Mankind's new jacket denoting the new fashion, which for him and his friends is idle living and idle language, symbolizes the state of his soul. Haukyn himself is connected with the abuse of rhetoric in that he lies, gossips, and uses his tongue as a weapon of revenge, thereby lending support to the suggestion of a literary influence in this case. Of course, Mischief and his friends behave much as Haukyn behaves by using such language against Mercy when they mock him and imitate his language. The Bible says that words reflect the state of one's heart and soul; therefore, words take on added importance in a morality play, a fact readily displayed in the rhetoric theme.

The playwright continues to display his own rhetorical virtuosity in his imagery. Each time a major image is used, it will reflect a different angle of one or both of the principle themes or one of the supporting thematic motifs. For example, the horse image is introduced by Mercy as a proverb depicting the essence of his speech on moderation. The proverb states that an overfed horse will not obey his master and will likely throw the master into the mud. Symbolically, the horse represents Mankind who can overindulge in the sensual pleasures of life, causing him to throw off God's sovereignty. The horse-master metaphor is a common one for the body-soul dichotomy. The fleshly desires of the body can gain the upper hand and throw the soul into the mud, thereby tying into the essence of the scatological humor, which pictures the soul splattered with the filth of sin. These two images are adroitly joined to support the sovereignty theme from two angles at once. This horse image ties into the husband-wife image, which is used initially to introduce the sovereignty theme in the action of the play and which possibly was influenced by Chaucer's *The Canterbury Tales*. New Gyse says that he has fed his wife so well that she is the master, and she beats him. The husband-wife image reveals sovereignty from the domestic angle and begins with Nowadays and his wife Rachell. The language and imagery of this episode seem quite possibly to have been inspired by some of *The Canterbury Tales* dealing with the theme of domestic sovereignty. The body-soul image is introduced by Mankind as he laments his sensual nature's ability to overrule his soul. Mankind also unites this image with the husband-wife image in his initial speech by remarking that the husband will be sorry if the wife gains control in a metaphorical reference to the situation between his body and his soul. Mercy warns Mankind that idle living will allow Mischief to put a "bridle" on him, thus invoking the horse image. The playwright uses common images to support his themes but folds them into and over each other much like the pleats of a skirt, which unfold to reveal different views of the material and expand to increase the surface of the whole while maintaining their connection. The horse metaphor, the body-soul dichotomy, and the husband-wife image all turn on the reversal of the natural order of things, thus tying these major images into Mercy's judicial oration condemning New Gyse and his pals as being worse than beasts because they violate the natural order of things. The scatolo-gical scenes in which Mischief and Nought befoul themselves graphically put these villains in the category of beasts, further supporting Mercy's contention. Such rhetorical maneuvering underscores the idea at the heart of the play that one must be God's obedient servant or risk violating the natural order of things.

In addition to these major images, the author manages to squeeze several layers of meaning from his indirect comparison of Mankind to Job. Job's connection to rhetoric has been discussed, and his unquestioning obedience to God obviously supports the sovereignty theme. The fact that Gregory the Great reports that Job sat on a dunghill to remind himself of the filth of the flesh ties into the scatological humor; therefore, with one reference the author supports three major ideas in his play. Another example of this technique is the connection of Titivillus to rhetoric by literary tradition. Titivillus is the epitome of the villains in the tradition of sinister comedy which revolves around the idea of a diabolical game, and he is the adversary of God in the struggle for sovereignty over mankind's soul. The underlying metaphor and the two major themes are represented in one character.

After a concentrated study of the rhetoric of *Mankind*, it is safe to suggest that the early critics were hasty in labeling *Mankind* as a dirty play written for a rural audience. The highly sophisticated rhetorical techniques, the possibility of influence from *Piers Plowman* and *The Canterbury Tales*, along with the possibility of exposure to the teachings of Cicero and, perhaps, Quintilian, as well, indicate that Larry Clopper is probably correct in his opinion that the play was composed for an educated audience. *Mankind* is so well done, however, that its many layers of meaning would appeal to audiences of all educational levels during the Middle Ages. The author uses his ability with rhetoric to depict the Christian ideals of his themes in unfamiliar ways, using commonly-known proverbs and images creatively to stress the importance of God's sovereignty over Mankind from many different angles. The audience is bombarded with Christian doctrine, such as the need to avoid idle language and idle living, from many angles simultaneously in the multifaceted imagery, the rhetorical techniques, and the symbolism of the characters. The playwright very carefully fits all of the pieces into his dramatic puzzle. Mischief is not an extraneous character. As Titivillus's representative in the diabolical game, Mischief is an integral part of the action. Contrary to the opinion of a number of critics, Titivillus is more than appropriate as the Devil in this play, since he represents the three major aspects of the play—the game metaphor and the themes of sovereignty and rhetoric. The collection scene, which is often discussed as an intrusive element, is actually the initiating force for the liars' contest, as well as a symbol of the materialism and greed of New Gyse, Nowadays, and Nought. The scatological humor is vital to the structure of the play, since it graphically depicts the level of contamination of the souls of the Devil's minions, picturing the filth of sin for the audience, and supports the charge that the rogues are worse than animals in their behavior. The reference to Job and the use of the horse proverb weave this scatological humor into the fabric of the text, and, of course, the literary tradition of sinister comedy sets a precedent for the use of comedy with serious scenes. Since the playwright uses his skills with language to present the familiar tenets of Christian doctrine in unfamiliar and attention-getting ways and weaves all of the parts of his play together to form a coherent whole, his morality play, *Mankind*, is definitely a work of literary art based on the standards of Shklovsky and Barthes.

NOTES

[1]Since the Greek and the Latin names are the accepted form for the rhetorical terms, the intrusive device of underlining will be omitted in this study.

[2]Unless otherwise indicated all definitions of rhetorical terms are taken from Richard A. Lanham's *A Handlist of Rhetorical Terms*.

CHAPTER THREE

A Linguistic Approach to the Structure of *Mankind*

Faith was the cornerstone of medieval Christian theology. That faith, however, was continually jeopardized by social, political, and economic circumstances for which the emergence of the middle class, beginning in the twelfth century, was at least partly responsible. The middle class was pragmatic and had an outlook that tended toward the urban, national, and secular rather than toward the ecclesiastical (Artz 228). A strong belief in God and the Christian religion was necessary if one were to keep his sights set on heaven and to avoid the snares of the material world of the Devil. Given man's basic human nature, such avoidance was not easy, even before the approach of the Renaissance heralded a change in the world focus. A late fifteenth-century English morality play, *Mankind* is poised on the brink of a new world view which would exalt humanity rather than God and the play reflects in its structure the reality of the threat to the soul posed by the steady encroachment of middle class materialism and the consequences of failure to take action against a weak faith. A linguistic analysis of the structure of *Mankind* based loosely on the ideas of modern critical theorists Claude Levi-Strauss and Tzvetan Todorov, coupled with the basic processes involved in transformational grammar and adapted for use with the drama, will reveal the literary artistry of the author as he creatively attempts to remind the audience of this insidious spiritual danger inherent in ordinary daily life.

When Levi-Strauss was doing research on myths from Australia, he discovered that a major structural principle was the classification by pairs of opposites (Totemism 88). According to Levi-Strauss, the mind has a natural tendency to classify a totality in very general and abstract terms, thereby putting the complexities of the reality of a situation through "a series of progressive purifications" until that situation can be understood in the form of a simple binary opposition, such as peace and war or black and white (*The Savage Mind* 217). Once the human mind has broken down a total situation into these simple concepts, it can proceed to understand the more difficult aspects involved in the reality of that situation. For the people in the Middle Ages a "war between Good and Evil was the profoundest reality of life, since upon the issue hung the eternal destiny of the soul" (Schmitt 24). This struggle between Good and Evil appears in *Mankind* in the form of a binary opposition that is the foundation for the structure of the play. This deep structural element manifests itself in the surface structure of the play as various dichotomies and images.

Although the opposition between Good and Evil is the primary contrast in the deep structure of *Mankind*, this binary pair is also an important part of the surface structure of the play. According to Todorov, the basic plot of a narrative evolves in the passage from one equilibrium to a second equilibrium that is similar but not exactly the same as the first equilibrium. A power or force of some sort disrupts the stability of the equilibrium, creating a state of disequilibrium. A force or power moving in the opposite direction

A Linguistic Approach to the Structure of *Mankind* 133

restores the equilibrium (Todorov 111). In the view of A. J. Greimas the movement from one opposition of a binary pair to the other opposition involves the transference on the surface structure of some entity, such as a quality or an object, from one actant to another, and this movement is the heart of narrative (Hawkes 90).

Even though Todorov and Greimas were referring to narrative in their descriptions of plot structure, the system will work with drama, and when applied to *Mankind* will reveal the basic movement from Good to Evil and back to Good again. Levi-Strauss's ideas on binary opposition and Todorov's theories concerning minimal plot structure can be used in an analysis of *Mankind* with little or no adaptation, because the notion of story is similar in narrative and drama. The texts of narrative and drama are quite different, however, and Todorov's system of narrative transformations, propositions, sequences, and moods must be changed to fit the needs of drama in order to shed light on how the language of the play functions in relation to the structure. For the purposes of this analysis of the linguistic structure of *Mankind*, the terms used by Todorov will be used with modifications for dramatic action. Although Todorov's basic system has been explained in Chapter One and presented in detail in Appendix A, a brief review of the definitions will be useful at this point.

Todorov points out that his ideas concerning narrative transformations and other aspects of the grammar of narrative are based on "the perspective of a logical and universal grammar, not that of a particular language" (225). As a result of this disclaimer, Todorov is not hampered by the rules of a specific language and is able to turn his attention to the function of language in general. Propositions in Todorov's system represent distinct actions in the plot and consist of a subject and a predicate, corresponding to the agent and the action of the particular element of the plot involved. Todorov defines *sequence* as two distinct and separate situations which can each be described by a few propositions (232). This definition is a refinement of Shklovsky's, which labels the sequence as an action and its corresponding reaction (Todorov 232). Mood is an important secondary grammatical category in Todorov's grammar of narrative, because the mood of the proposition defines the relationship between the subject and the proposition (113). He lists five moods: indicative, obligative, optative, conditional and predictive. Although Todorov's definition of transformation is similar to that found in modern linguistic theory, his version is actually much less restricted and technical than the definitions found in texts on transformational grammar. In Todorov's view a relationship of transformation exists between two propositions "when one predicate remains identical on both sides" (224). Simple transformations involve one subject and one predicate, whereas complex transformations involve two predicates and either one or two subjects. Todorov lists six simple transformations (mode, intention, result, manner, aspect, status) and six complex transformations (appearance, knowledge, description, supposition, subjectivation, attitude) (Todorov 225-30). Todorov summarizes the plot of a narrative, breaks the action into propositions, and analyzes the propositions to determine what transformations have occurred. Sequences are composed of the propositions, and a narrative tale may have one or more sequences in its plotline.

Although Todorov's method of analysis was originally designed for use with the language of narrative, the method can be applied to the language of morality plays, even though the action of a drama is occurring in the "here and now" between an "I/speaker" and a "you/addressee listener" rather than being described by a narrator. The text of a morality play such as *Mankind* reflects the action taking place between the characters. Using the language of the text as a basis, one can discern the kind of action occurring between the characters without the benefit of an actual dramatic presentation with live actors, who can distort the play somewhat with individual interpretations. The predicates of the texts, especially the main verbs, indicate the type of action that the playwright intended. The concrete verbal structures in the text then represent some abstract verbal quality (the abstract verb) in the deep structure. For example, Mercy might be warning, accusing, or complimenting Mischief, and that verbal quality will be expressed in the actual verbs, auxiliaries, adverbs, and other modifying parts of the predicates in the text. Any word in the predicate regardless of its technical classification in English grammar is considered to be part of the concrete verbal structure of the text if that word sheds light on the action taking place. Once the abstract verb is discerned from the language of the text, that specific component of the action of the plot can be described in a proposition. For instance, in lines 124–25 New Gyse speaks to Mercy: "Ey, ey! Yowr body ys full of Englysch Laten. / I am aferde yt wyll brest." New Gyse is telling Mercy that Mercy's body is so full of English Latin that New Gyse fears it will explode. These lines become the proposition: New Gyse accuses Mercy of pomposity in language. Supporting this proposition from the deep structure is the abstract verb *accuse*. The interaction of the characters can thus be seen as one level and the actual verbal exchange in the text as another. Both levels are necessary to the proper formulation of a proposition in a drama. Todorov's narrative propositions become, in this analysis of *Mankind*, propositions based on the verbal structures derived from the important actions of the plotline. Underlying these propositions, which summarize and describe the actions in the play, are the abstract verbs in the deep structure which denote the action taking place. The I/speaker of the interaction of characters involved in the proposition is the subject of that proposition.

The term *deep structure* in this context is similar to that found in transformational grammar in that the abstract verbs must go through the process of transformation in order to become the propositions that evolve from the concrete words of the surface structure. Despite the similarity in the operational process, the term *deep structure* does not mean exactly the same thing in this study of the structure of *Mankind* as it means in modern linguistic theory. In this study, the term refers to the abstract and somewhat nebulous area from which the dramatic construct evolves. The dramatic construct includes both the linguistic structures that form the actual text of the play and the kind of action occurring between the characters involved in each proposition. The deep structure in this sense is the vague, indistinct area in which the ideas of the playwright concerning the actions of the plot first achieve a kind of form. The text, which is the dramatic construct, is the final form. Since action is the essence of drama, determination of the abstract verbs in the deep structure is essential to a valid analysis of the linguistic structure of a dramatic text. When the abstract verb establishes the kind of action going on between the characters, the propositions can then be set up and analyzed to determine the types of transformations that have occurred.

As in Todorov's theory these propositions form sequences; however, in a dramatic analysis it is more convenient to have a sequence refer to the interaction of characters in a specific situation rather than to two separate actions resembling an action and its reaction. Todorov's definition works well with a general summary of the plot of a folk tale in which the entire story may be some form of action and reaction, but the definition is not suitable for the more detailed summary of the action of *Mankind*, which is far more complicated than the average folk tale. Since the sequence deals with the specific interaction of characters concerned with a certain topic of conversation or a single situation, it changes when the character alignment or the focus of the situation changes. For example, the interaction between Mercy and Mankind at the end of the first scene ends with the exit of Mercy and the entrance of New Gyse, Nowadays and Nought (hereafter referred to as the Three N's for brevity's sake). A new sequence begins with the interaction of Mankind and the Three N's. In addition to the change in characters, the change in the focus of the situation creates a new sequence within the same character interaction as in the interaction between Mercy and the Three N's in lines 72–161. The first sequence concerns the topic of dancing and merrymaking and includes four propositions. The second sequence concerns the topic of rhetoric or the use of language and includes nine propositions. Each time a character directly speaks to the audience, the situation is considered to be an interaction between the character and the audience and is judged to be a separate sequence. Technically, such a situation is normally viewed as a dramatic monologue; however, a very close relationship existed between the medieval audience and the performance of a morality play, a fact previously noted by scholars such as David Bevington (15), and supported by the numerous apostrophes and other forms of direct address in the text. Although the audience speaks no written dialogue, medieval people tended to consciously participate in what they perceived (Schmitt 25). Schmitt points out that "the idea of objectivity, of the existence of things the identity of which can be known quite apart from ourselves, is a product of a scientific rationalist age; it is not a medieval idea" (25). Both the audience and the actors would have considered the audience part of the drama, participating in some fashion in the unfolding action; therefore, the dramatic monologues in *Mankind* are more appropriately categorized as interactions with the audience in this context.

In *Mankind* sequences combine to yield episodes. Episodes are composed of two or more sequences dealing with the same idea or motif. For instance, the two sequences involving the interaction between Mercy and Mischief and that between Mercy and the Three N's in the first scene form the episode of the Confrontation between Good and Evil, which is the binary opposition that supports the structure of the play. (Todorov uses the term *episode* in his theory, but his definition concerns the states of equilibrium and disequilibrium and has no bearing on the method of analysis employed in this study of *Mankind*.)

Todorov also makes a distinction between simple and complex transformations that is not essential in a study of drama. The meanings of the individual transformations are more important in a dramatic analysis than the number of subjects and predicates involved in the propositions, which is the important factor in distinguishing between complex and simple transformations in a narrative analysis. Since action is the foundation of the drama, the transformation (or transformations) that best describes what has occurred in the proposition is the most important consideration. In many instances Todorov's designated number of subjects and predicates appears in the proper transformations, but on many occasions the dramatic situation does not coincide with the formula of a narrative situation. For example, in Mercy's opening speech the proposition yielded by the first two lines is: Mercy tells the audience that God ought to be glorified. Mercy, the I/speaker, is the subject of the proposition and the audience, the you/listener-addressee, is the object. The abstract verb in the deep structure is *tell*, or possibly *teach* because Christian doctrine is involved here. Since Mercy is imparting knowledge to the audience, or reminding them of known doctrine, the transformation of description describes the dramatic action of the proposition. The message is that the audience should take action and glorify God. When "the possibility, the impossibility, or the necessity of an action" is involved, the transformation of mode has occurred (Todorov 226). The first proposition in *Mankind*, therefore, requires both a complex and a simple transformation in order to fully describe the situation in this dramatic construct. The complex transformation of description depicts the level of the interaction of Mercy and the audience based on the abstract verb *tell* or *teach*, whereas the simple transformation of mode relates to the linguistic message of the dramatic construct. Since both levels are needed to adequately display the structure of *Mankind* and to understand how the language functions in that structure, Todorov's specifications regarding simple and complex transformations cannot be totally incorporated into the analysis.

Todorov's transformation of description is one of the most important transformations in the analysis of *Mankind*, because this transformation relates well to portraying the action between an I/speaker and a you/addressee-listener. These transformations deal with actions that "provoke knowledge" in the you/listener (Todorov 228). Todorov says that these transformations involve " 'verbs of speech,' " such as *to explain, to recount, to say* (228). Todorov's transformation conveys knowledge about something that has already happened. The transformation of description used in this study occurs when one character seeks to inform another about a previously unknown bit of knowledge, to remind him of something he has known in the past, or to give advice and directions on behavior. The transformation of description is thus the most basic transformation in the propositions of the dramatic construct.

The remaining transformations in Todorov's system are used in the analysis of *Mankind* in much the same form as he discusses them in *The Poetics of Prose* (226–30), except for the previously discussed stipulation regarding the subjects and predicates of simple and complex transformations. The transformation of knowledge is the counterpart to the transformation of description in that this transformation deals with knowledge provoked in the subject (I/speaker) instead of the object (you/addressee-listener). The transformation of supposition deals with predictions, whereas the transformation of intention concerns the actual plans and intentions of the subject of the proposition. The two transformations are important in the linguistic structure as unifying components. For instance, Mercy predicts that Titivillus will deceive Mankind with lies and his net, which actually happens in the second scene. In Todorov's terminology this action and its reaction form a sequence, the heart of a folk tale; however, in the morality play this action and its reaction are simply connecting units in the overall structure. The same situation holds true for announcements of intentions which are soon carried out in the play. The transformation of subjectivation concerns the attitude of the I/speaker and what he thinks or believes about a situation. The belief of the subject is what is important, not whether the thing that he believes is true or false. The transformation of attitude expresses the attitude of the subject of the proposition based on a value judgment made by the subject about a situation. This transformation is often found in conjunction with the transformation of description in *Mankind*. For instance, a compliment or an accusation involves both the value judgment and verb of speech, as Todorov points out in his remarks concerning transformations (230). The transformation of mode involves the necessity or the impossibility of an action and is often found in *Mankind* along with the transformation of description. The transformation of intention concerns the subject's plans to do something, whereas the transformation of result deals with actions that have already been completed. The transformation of manner represents the way in which an action occurs. Transformations of aspect represent the aspect of the verb such as the inchoative (*begin*), the progressive (*be in the act of*), and the termination (*finish*), which are pertinent to the analysis of *Mankind*. The transformation of appearance conveys deception of some sort and generally deals with the opposite of what is actually taking place.

Todorov's system of transformations does not include all of the operations necessary for an analysis of the action of *Mankind*; therefore, a few additional transformations formulated along the lines of some of the basic operations in transformational grammar were included in the method of analysis employed with the morality play. The transformation of negation is self-explanatory. As such this name is deemed more suitable for this study than "transformation of status," which handles the negative form in Todorov's system. The transformation of command is, however, a new transformation. Numerous instances arise in *Mankind* when Mercy or some other character tells another character to do or not to do something in such strong language that a transformation of description falls short of adequately categorizing the action. A transformation of command fills in the gap in these situations. The transformation of request is also an extra transformation, covering interrogative situations or situations in which one character seeks to provoke an action in another character. Such an action can be a simple reply to a question or a direct physical act. The transformation of request is indicated by such verbs as *ask, beg, beseech, request,* and *implore.* Another transformation that is essential to the analysis of the linguistic structure of *Mankind* is the transformation of analogy. The transformation of analogy concerns the metaphors and other images of the play. This transformation generally occurs in conjunction with the transformation of description. Metaphors and other such figures have their roots in the abstract verbs of the deep structure, even though metaphors are usually composed of nouns. When metaphors appear in the surface structure, at least two transformations must occur in the deep structure. First the action of comparison must be considered. To draw an analogy the playwright yokes two things together that are essentially different but are similar in an area that will symbolically strengthen the impact of the message of the actual words in the text. Two different things are thus mingled through the process of the transformation of analogy and become a symbolic image. Second, that image is imparted to the audience, as well as to the other characters involved, by the subject of the proposition through the transformation of description, which allows the listeners to gain knowledge about both the action occurring in the proposition and the larger meaning of the words themselves.

Along with the additional transformations, an extra mood must be added to the moods described by Todorov and a definition adjusted to fit dramatic action. Four of Todorov's moods have been discussed already in Chapter One and are useful in this study as they stand. One mood has not been discussed—the indicative mood. Todorov says that the indicative mood deals with what is real and concerns actions that have already happened (113). In English grammar the indicative mood indicates the plain or the factual. This analysis combines the two definitions in order to give the indicative mood the broader range necessary for dramatic action. The indicative mood then refers to both statements of fact and to actions that have been completed. The extra mood that seems to be useful in the analysis of *Mankind* is the imperative mood which signifies an action that is commanded or urgently requested, as well as an action that must occur. This mood often is found in propositions containing transformations of command and occasionally in those containing transformations of mode.

These additions, changes, and substitutions in Todorov's system of moods, transformations, propositions, and sequences create a useful method of analyzing the important verbal structures of the plot of *Mankind*. When this method of analysis is combined with Levi-Strauss's binary oppositions and the minimal plot structure of equilibrium-disequilibrium-equilibrium, a more complete

A Linguistic Approach to the Structure of *Mankind*   143

picture of the linguistic structure of *Mankind* emerges. The binary opposition of Good versus Evil—which many critics have seen as the basic conflict in morality plays—becomes the major structural principle in *Mankind* from which the primary images and other important dichotomies emerge.

Technically, Mercy's opening speech is part of the initial state of equilibrium, as well as part of the framework surrounding the action of the play; however, the opposition between Good and Evil appears in this speech and is the foundation of the first major image in the play, with which Mercy culminates his speech. The detailed information from the analysis of the structure of this speech is compiled in a chart in the appendix to this study, but a brief summary reveals the major focus of the speech. Mercy represents God on earth, and he warns the audience about God's opponent, the Devil; hence the forces of Good and Evil are delineated before the action begins. Mercy's speech yields twenty-two propositions based on seven abstract verbs: *tell (teach, inform,* or similar verbs), *warn, advise, command, beg, ask,* and *compare.* The speech alternates between flat statements of Christian doctrine and directions to the audience based on Christian doctrine concerning actions they should take and what actions they should avoid. Toward the end of his remarks, Mercy uses imagery to make his words more concrete and relevant. The final image is the corn-chaff image, which telegraphs the idea that the good people will be saved and the evil people will be damned to the fires of hell. The transformation of description appears in almost every proposition, since Mercy, the I/speaker, is teaching the audience, the you/addressee, how to behave if they wish to be included in the corn half of the image. Mercy uses three apostrophes and the pronoun *you* on several occasions, which create the illusion of interaction and make the audience part of the drama from the beginning. The transformation of mode, which deals with the necessity of performing some action, appears in seven propositions. Mercy's five images emerge from the abstract verb *compare* in the deep structure and the transformation of analogy.

The overt clash between Good and Evil does not occur in *Mankind* until Mischief enters the scene to begin the action with Mercy (11. 45–70). During this interaction with Mercy, Mischief hooks into Mercy's corn metaphor in order to mock Mercy and to present creatively the idea of opposition. The abstract verbal quality of mocking manifests itself in two propositions:

> Mischief commands Mercy to stop his chattering about corn and chaff.
>
> Mischief tells Mercy that he has hired (on as) a corn thresher.

The first proposition involves the transformation of command and the imperative mood, whereas the second employs the transformation of description, the transformation of analogy, and the indicative mood. By "corn thresher" Mischief intends both the literal and the symbolic meaning; therefore, transformation of analogy is needed. Mischief openly sets up the opposition between Good and Evil in the surface structure when he refers to the fact that Mercy ordered him to leave in God's name not the Devil's; therefore, Mischief, a loyal servant of the Devil, plans to stay (11. 69–71). Of course, Mischief eventually leaves, but the missing manuscript sheet leaves the exact circumstances of the departure unknown. Mischief lays down the rules of the opposition when he tells Mercy the reason for his appearance in this proposition: Mischief tells Mercy that he has come to make Mercy a game (1. 69). The binary opposition between Good and Evil in the deep structure expresses itself in the surface plotline as the game metaphor that controls the action among the characters. This proposition and the proposition detailing Mischief's plans to stay both use the transformations of description and intention and the predictive mood. For Mischief's half of this sequence with Mercy, the most important abstract verbs are *mock* and *oppose*. The transformation of intention serves Mischief best in this sequence, since he plans to oppose Mercy in this "game."

Mercy has certainly not remained quiet throughout this exchange. Most of Mercy's propositions in this sequence seem to be reactions to the sudden threat presented by Mischief. Mercy questions Mischief about the reasons for his appearance, tells him that he is not wanted, orders him to leave on foot, and other things of a similar nature. The most important proposition of which Mercy is the subject in this sequence with Mischief is the following: Mercy accuses Mischief of disruptive behavior (ll. 64–65). The transformation of knowledge occurs here, because Mercy realizes that it is Mischief who has interrupted his lovely speech. The transformation of attitude plays a role in this proposition, because accusations require value judgments. Since both the knowledge gained and the value judgment must be passed to Mischief, the transformation of description is also employed. Although Mercy speaks of a specific disruptive behavior on the part of Mischief in the text, the accusation of the proposition is proved to be true in a general sense in the play, since Mischief intends to be disruptive and to interrupt Mercy's powerful rhetoric in order to win Mankind's soul. Even though the proposition does not fit exactly Todorov's requirements for the predictive mood, the abstract verb *accuse* is in the predictive mood in this context, because it reaches into the action of the play beyond this sequence in the manner of a prediction or a foreshadowing of things to come.

This initial sequence involving Mercy and Mischief in a verbal exchange is part of the larger structural component, the episode.

This episode is the confrontation between Good and Evil and includes two more sequences in addition to the Mercy-Mischief interaction. These sequences concern the interaction between Mercy and the Three N's (11. 72–161). This character interaction does not change with regard to character alignment, but the focus of the situation changes. In the first sequence the propositions of which the Three N's are the subject revolve around attempts to get Mercy to dance and to join their merrymaking. The propositions of which Mercy is the subject concern Mercy's refusal to dance and his attempts to get the rowdies to stop their noise. The second sequence deals with the topic of language. Mercy's most important proposition in this sequence concerns an implied prediction that would not be lost on a medieval audience: Mercy warns the Three N's that idle language is dangerous (1. 47). The transformations of description and attitude are present in this transformation. Implicit in a warning is the idea that some consequence will occur if the situation is not changed. Although the dangers of idle language can be considered a flat statement of fact in the indicative mood, in this context the predictive mood is more appropriate. Most of the propositions directed by the Three N's involve mocking or accusing in some way. One proposition is worthy of note: New Gyse accuses Mercy of pomposity in language (1. 124). The transformations of description and attitude transpire in this proposition, which is in the indicative mood. Mercy is, after all, a bit pompous.

Often the boundaries of the sequence coincide with those of the episode in *Mankind*. Mercy's judicial oration (11. 162–85) in which Good denounces Evil is such an instance. This sequence is another interaction between Mercy and the audience; however, in the opening speech Mercy only acknowledges the presence of Evil and warns against the Devil. In this sequence he openly condemns the Three N's, the representatives of Evil, for their language and their lifestyle. Mercy's aggression indicates a realization on his part that the threat from Evil is strong.

These two episodes are part of the initial state of equilibrium in the structure of the play, but the third episode reveals the definition of that equilibrium. This episode concerns Mankind's confrontation with Good and contains two sequences. The first sequence is Mankind's interaction with the audience (11. 186-216). In that sequence Mankind introduces the body-soul image, which evolves from the Good-Evil binary opposition in the deep structure and becomes the most important surface manifestation of that dichotomy. The body-soul image depicts the internal struggle between Good and Evil that continues within Mankind until he dies. This internal tug-of-war reflects the external conflict between Good, represented by Mercy, and Evil, represented by Mischief and his cohorts, for the soul of Mankind. Most of the propositions in this sequence describe the anguish Mankind feels over this battle between his flesh and his soul for control of his being. The major transformations are those of description and attitude and the mood is usually indicative, except for the proposition in which Mankind asks Mercy for his help with the internal battle. This proposition uses the transformation of request and the optative mood, which reflects the desires of the subject of the proposition. The second sequence is Mankind's interaction with Mercy (11. 217-309). The most important proposition in this sequence occurs when Mercy defines the equilibrium: Mercy tells Mankind that there is always a battle between the body and the soul (1. 227). This proposition involves the transformation of description and the transformation of aspect, because the battle is continuous. The mood is indicative, because Mercy is relaying a statement of fact. The normal situation for Mankind on earth is the war between the natural desires of his body for worldly gratification and the higher inclination of his soul for spiritual pursuits. In order to maintain this initial state of equilibrium, Mankind must keep a balance between the two factions, with the soul (Good) having a measure of control. Many of Mercy's propositions in this sequence concern his advice to Mankind on how to avoid vice, thereby allowing virtue to maintain control of the constant tension between Good and Evil. These propositions often echo those in the opening speech, which reflect Christian doctrine on proper behavior. Mercy's message to Mankind and, indirectly, to the audience is to use moderation in all things; therefore, the initial equilibrium is characterized by moderation. An excessive lifestyle is evil. Three of Mercy's propositions should be noted in this context:

>Mercy commands Mankind to resist temptation.

>Mercy commands Mankind to oppress his spiritual enemy.

>Mercy tells Mankind to be Christ's own knight.

The first two propositions employ the transformation of command and the imperative mood, which underscores the urgency of the situation. The transformations of description and analogy appear in the third proposition, which is in the optative mood. By comparing Mankind to the knights of old, Mercy introduces an image that emphasizes the messages of resisting temptation and oppressing the Devil in the first two propositions. Strong, unswerving faith is essential in the fight against temptation. Knights, representatives of the best of mankind, often were afflicted by a faith that was insufficient to oppress the temptations of the flesh. Mercy is warning Mankind to be a strong faithful follower of Christ in order to win the struggle raging in his body between Good and Evil.

In addition to the knight image, Mercy introduces another image to strengthen his advice to Mankind to avoid excess in all things. Mercy uses the horse-rider image, which is a common symbol for the body and soul in the Middle Ages, to depict the dangers of an immoderate lifestyle. An overfed horse throws his master into the mud. A body that indulges in sensual pleasures of the world will throw off the controlling restraints of the soul. The binary opposition of Good-Evil underlies the horse-rider image through the analogy with the body-soul image.

Although not presented as an image, another example of the representation in the surface text of the binary opposition between Good and Evil in the deep structure is the symbolic contrast between Christianity and the occult. After Mercy leaves in the first scene, Mankind writes something on a piece of paper, which he attaches to his chest. The purpose of this badge is the defense of Mankind from superstitious charms (11. 315-21). In the sequence between Mischief and the Three N's at the beginning of the second scene, Mischief offers to cure the injuries of the whining men by cutting off the various body parts and then replacing them again. In order to chop off a head and replace it successfully, Mischief would need magical powers. The Three N's are skeptical and refuse Mischief's offer. These two sequences, therefore, contain references to the world of the occult, which form a sharp contrast to the Christian doctrine all around them. The most important transformations in both sequences are those of description and intention. The transformation of negation appears in the propositions dealing with the refusals of each of the Three N's to allow Mischief to chop off anything.

One of Mercy's propositions deals obliquely with the consequences of failure to resist temptation: Mercy tells Mankind that if he wants to be crowned, he must fight (1. 231). This proposition yields the transformations of description, mode, and supposition. The mood is the conditional. Mankind will not go to heaven if he fails to fight temptation, an idea found in a number of Mercy's

150   A Diabolical Game to Win Man's Soul

propositions in *Mankind*. Although this is one of Mercy's predictions based on doctrine that cannot come true until Mankind dies, some of his other predictions are verified by the action of the play, thereby enhancing the truth of those predictions that continue beyond the play, and strengthening the audience's faith in the process.

Most of Mercy's predictions that come true later in the play concern propositions that warn Mankind to beware of the Three N's, who will try to pervert his good habits, and to beware of Titivillus, who will become invisible, whisper in Mankind's ear, and use his net to blind him. All of these propositions are in the predictive mood and reveal the transformations of description, attitude, and supposition. These predictions and their fulfillment create connecting bonds within the play's structure. Another of Mercy's predictions that influences the play's structure indirectly is the following: Mercy tells Mankind that God will test him for constancy (1. 283). This prediction allows Mankind to indulge in pride at his victory over the Three N's later in the play. This situation sets in motion the forces that cause the disequilibrium in the plot.

The interaction between Mankind and the Three N's is the sequence in which the confrontation occurs. Mankind has informed the audience in the previous sequence that he intends to dig the earth. The transformation of intention along with the optative and predictive moods are important in these propositions: Mankind intends to dig with his spade; the Three N's try to distract Mankind from his work. Another important proposition in this sequence is the following: Mankind tells the Three N's that he must work, because it is his living (1. 350). The transformations are those of description and mode. The mood is conditional. This proposition includes the binary oppositions Life-Death and Idleness-Work, which emerge from the basic binary opposition of Good-Evil. Mankind lines up on the side of Good-Life-Work in this sequence when he realizes that working is important to both physical and spiritual living. The Three N's are on the opposing side of Evil-Death-Idleness. The most important propositions in the sequence concern the fight between Three N's and Mankind:

> Mankind succeeds in driving the Three N's away with his spade.
>
> Mankind thinks that God has tested him.
>
> Mankind believes that he has passed the test.

The first proposition employs the transformation of result, since Mankind has completed the action of driving the rogues away, and the indicative mood. The other two propositions concern the indicative mood and the transformation of subjectivation, which refers to the subject's belief in something; whether that something is true is not relevant to the transformation. Mankind's pleasure in his victory is in itself an indulgence in sensual pleasure and admits of personal pride. Pride has a tendency to shift one's focus from spiritual to worldly pursuits, unless one has the faith of the Pope. From this moment the stage is set for the movement toward the state of disequilibrium.

After the fight sequence between Mankind and the Three N's, the activity among the evil characters in *Mankind* increases. Mischief is distraught because Mankind has joined Mercy's side in the contest between Good and Evil, and has struck the Three N's blows with his spade. The forces of Evil begin to regroup and then take up a collection from the audience before reinforcements arrive in the person of the Devil himself, Titivillus. The propositions involved in these sequences reveal the shallowness and worldly orientation of the speakers. The major transformation is that of description, because the characters are mainly giving information to each other. The mood used most often is the indicative.

Once Titivillus enters the scene, the pace of the action increases, and the truth of Mercy is replaced by the lies of the Devil and his minions, which represents another dichotomy based on the Good-Evil binary opposition. The first sequence concerns Titivillus and the Three N's. Titivillus warns the audience that the Three N's are horse thieves. Titivillus then tests the rogues to prove their worthless nature to the audience. Titivillus commands each of the Three N's in turn to give him money. From the nature of the abstract verbs *warn* and *command* one can see the transformations of description and attitude, as well as that of command in the propositions. The only instances of the transformation of appearance in *Mankind* are found in the responses of the Three N's to Titivillus's request for money. Each pretends that he has no money. The derelicts even lie to their master. When the Three N's leave, Titivillus tells them to go their way in the Devil's name. This proposition, a kind of "blessing," is the negative side of the proposition in which Mercy blesses Mankind in God's name before Mercy exits in the first scene. The positive-negative dichotomy has its roots in the Good-Evil binary opposition underlying the play's structure. Another Titivillus proposition that is important in this sequence concerns his predictions. Just as Mercy makes predictions during the play, so does Titivillus, another parallel action of Good-Truth and Evil-Lies. The Three N's have complained about Mankind's behavior. Titivillus tells the Three N's that he will avenge their wounds. The transformations are those of description and intention, and the mood is predictive. This prediction comes true when Mankind defects to the side of Evil, thereby putting his soul in danger of damnation.

The next sequence consists of the interaction of Titivillus and the audience, which includes Titivillus's detailed plans to corrupt

Mankind and Titivillus's predictions concerning Mankind's behavior in response to the planned deceit. Titivillus tells the audience that he will test Mankind's good intentions in order to thwart them. Titivillus informs the audience of his plans to become invisible, to whisper lies to Mankind, to hang his net before Mankind's eyes, to place a board in the ground, and to contaminate the corn with weeds. Other propositions deal with forecasts about Mankind's anger and loss of patience when the ground is too hard to dig. The controlling transformations in addition to the obvious one of description are those of intention, when Titivillus's plans are involved, and of supposition, when Mankind's response is involved. The mood that prevails is the predictive.

In the sequence dealing with the interaction of Mankind and Titivillus (11. 541-606), Titivillus's predictions are realized and Mankind shifts to the side of Evil. Titivillus applies the force of lies to the situation and upsets the balance between Good and Evil in Mankind's soul. Evil gains the upper hand, creating the state of disequilibrium. To achieve this situation Titivillus must first wear down Mankind's formidable defenses, his willingness to work and his devotion to prayer as a symbol of his faith in God. Titivillus says on two occasions that he has come to "yrke" ("weary") Mankind (1. 532; 1. 556). The movement into the state of disequilibrium is not instantaneous but gradual. Mankind complains that the hard work makes him weary. This proposition based on the abstract verb *complains* indicates that Titivillus's hidden board is having the desired effect. The transformations are description and attitude. The mood is indicative. Mankind discovers that his corn is contaminated. This proposition yields the transformation of knowledge and the indicative mood. Mankind tells the audience that he will give up his spade forever. This proposition displays the transformations of description and intention in the predictive mood. This proposition reflects the unusual I/speaker and you/

addressee situation of Mankind's believing that he is speaking only to the audience, because Titivillus is invisible to him. Such a scene must have provoked much laughter in the Middle Ages. Unseen Evil silently corrupts a basically good man. Titivillus causes Mankind to interrupt his prayer service to attend to nature's call. The transformation of result becomes important in Titivillus's propositions informing the audience of how he separated Mankind from his prayers. These actions are not accomplished facts. Mankind has three propositions that illustrate the result of Titivillus's handiwork:

> Mankind tells the audience that he will behave differently now.

> Mankind tells the audience that he is almost weary of both labor and prayer.

> Mankind tells the audience that he will not labor or pray again.

The transformations involved in the first proposition are those of description and intention in the predictive mood. The transformations in the third proposition are those of description, intention, negation, and the mood is predictive. The second proposition includes the transformations of description, attitude, and aspect, and the mood is predictive. The transformation of attitude suggests a value judgment about his state has been made by Mankind; however, the transformation of aspect is used, because the verbal structure "is almost" ("nere yrke") (1. 585) indicates that the state is in process and has not been concluded permanently. Mercy still stands in the way, but Titivillus remedies that situation by sending Mankind a dream that Mercy was hanged as a horse thief. Titivillus

A Linguistic Approach to the Structure of *Mankind*   155

also tells Mankind in the dream that he must seek forgiveness from the Three N's and listen to their advice. All of Titivillus's lies in this context are transformations of description and the mood is indicative. If the propositions are formulated from Mankind's point of view the transformations are those of subjectivation since Mankind believes the dream to be true. Transformations make no distinction between lies and truth, except the transformation of knowledge in the situation in which the subject learns or realizes that the action was deceitful. Titivillus exits aware of the fact that Mankind believes the dream. Titivillus tells the audience that his game is done and that he has brought Mankind to mischief and shame. This situation reflects the transformation of result, because Mankind has been worn down and has changed sides in the game between Good and Evil. The action shifts into the state of disequilibrium as a result of Titivillus's lies and deceit.

The state of disequilibrium mirrors the initial state of equilibrium in that Mankind now worships Evil as he had previously worshipped Good. This situation can be seen in the lines of the text from the two sections of the play which parallel each other. In the first scene when Mankind struggles with the forces of Good and Evil within his own soul, he asks Mercy for help. After he wakes from his Titivillus-inspired dream in the second scene, he seeks forgiveness and counsel from the Three N's:

Mankind's words to Mercy:

> All heyll, semely father! ȝe be welcom to þis house.
> (1. 209)
> My body wyth my soull ys ever querulose.
> I prey yow, for sent charyte, of yowr supportacyon.
> (11. 211–12)

156   A Diabolical Game to Win Man's Soul

> I beseche yow hertyly of yowr gostly [spiritual] comforte.
>
> (1. 213)

Mankind's words to the Three N's:

> ȝe be welcum, New Gyse! Ser, what chere wyth yow?
>
> (1. 625)
>
> I aske mercy of New Gyse, Nowadays and Nought.
>
> (1. 650)
>
> Now, I prey yow hertyly of yowr goode wyll.
>
> (1. 657)
>
> I crye yow mercy of all þat I dyde amysse.
>
> (1. 658)

Mercy's response to Mankind's appeal for help is similar to Nought's response to Mankind's appeal for pardon and good will:

> MERCY: Stonde wppe on yowr fete, I prey yow aryse.
>
> (1. 218)
>
> NOUGHT: Stonde wppe on yowr feet! why stonde ȝe so styll?
>
> (1. 661)

Mercy's command, uttered in the initial state of equilibrium, parallels the structure of Nought's, uttered in the state of disequilibrium, a situation which points up a Positive-Negative dichotomy rooted in the basic Good-Evil binary pair of the deep structure. Further evidence of the mirror image of the two states can be seen in the contrasting advice given to Mankind from Mercy and from Mischief and the Three N's:

> MERCY: Cyrst sende yow goode comforte! ȝe
> be welcum, my frende.
> (1. 217)
>
> MISCHIEF: Mankynde, cum hethere! God sende
> yow þe gowte [gout]!
> (1. 702)

Mercy opens his advice on how to avoid vice with a plea to Christ to send comfort to Mankind, which is both positive and good. Mercy's advice counsels directly God's sovereignty and moderation in all things. The primary abstract verbs supporting Mercy's propositions are *fight, resist, suppress, intend* and *serve*. Mischief, however, opens his advice on how to behave licentiously and illegally with a plea to God to give Mankind the gout, which is both negative and evil. The gout may be an appropriate disease in this context, since this disease sometimes is associated with a life of excess, although the tendency to the disease is actually hereditary. Mischief, of course, advocates a life of excess to the point of criminality in the mock court sequence. Mischief's advice, therefore, counsels implicitly the Devil's sovereignty and an excessive lifestyle, overindulgence in sensual pleasures, and worldly pursuits. Mischief and the Three N's initiate Mankind into Evil in the mock court sequence (667-733) by forcing him to answer "I wyll ser" after each direction to commit adultery, to drink at the alehouse, to avoid religious rituals, and similar things. The major abstract verbs in these propositions are *commit, rob, steal, kill, avoid,* and *attack*. Before Mankind is initiated, Nought points out (1. 669) that Mankind is "on of owr men," an acknowledgement that the disequilibrium is now achieved.

When total disequilibrium is reached and Mankind has the

new jacket symbolizing his new worldly status, the forces of Good in the form of Mercy become increasingly active. Mercy enters at the end of the second scene commanding Mankind to flee the company of the evil rogues, but Mankind avoids a confrontation by stalling Mercy with a promise to talk later. The third scene opens with Mercy's long lament concerning Mankind's defection. The most important proposition in this sequence is the one depicting Mercy's resolution to make his next move in this game for Mankind's soul: Mercy tells the audience that he will find Mankind. The transformation of intention and the predictive mood are the primary elements of this proposition. This is another of Mercy's predictions that comes true in the play. Mischief and the Three N's realize the threat Mercy poses to their victory. They devise a plan to win the game by having Mankind kill himself in his unrepentant state. The devil will get his soul in such a case. The most important proposition in this sequence occurs when New Gyse tells the others that Mankind will kill himself when he hears that Mercy seeks him. The major transformation is that of supposition and the mood is predictive. This prediction almost comes true, but Mercy arrives in time to stop Mankind from committing suicide; such a timely arrival is itself rather symbolic, given the context of the play.

    The movement back toward a new equilibrium begins with Mercy's resolve to search for Mankind and progresses in earnest when Mercy finds Mankind. Mankind's pride, which allowed the process to begin, stands in the way of the establishment of a new state of equilibrium. Mankind tells Mercy that he is unworthy to see Mercy's consoling face. This proposition yields the transformations of description, attitude, and negation along with the indicative mood. Mercy tells Mankind that if Mankind will meekly ask for Mercy, he will agree. This proposition displays the transformations of description and intention and the conditional mood. Several of Mercy's propositions inform Mankind in different ways that he must voluntarily obey God. These propositions have the transformation of description and the optative mood. Mankind is outraged that he must ask for mercy again. This proposition contains the transformations of attitude and mode and the indicative mood. Several of Mankind's propositions offer excuses in various guises. These propositions are characterized by the transformations of description and attitude and the indicative mood. Mercy uses many tools of persuasion on Mankind. One proposition refers to the body-soul image by pointing out that Mankind must ask for mercy while the two parts are still joined. Mercy's truth finally prevails: Mankind at long last tells Mercy that Mercy is worthy to have his love. This proposition's most essential transformation is that of attitude because the fact that Mankind makes a value judgment concerning Mercy's worthiness rather than his own, as his actual words indicated earlier, reveals that Mankind's secular self at that point in the action does not choose to believe Mercy and does not want to give up worldly pursuits just yet. Another mirror image evolves here in Mankind's words which meant to him the opposite of what he was saying aloud to Mercy. It was Mercy Mankind was judging to be undesirable and unworthy, not himself. Mankind's propositions from this point display the transformation of knowledge in that Mankind realizes how Titivillus has tricked him with his invisibility, his lies, and his net. Mercy then warns Mankind again about Titivillus and the temptations of the world and the flesh. The important proposition in this context is the one that ties the body-soul image once again to the Good-Evil opposition: Mercy tells Mankind that the desires of his body brought him to Mischief. Mercy then blesses Mankind and sends him out in the world again. In this new state of equilibrium the tension between Good and Evil both within Mankind's soul and between God and the Devil will continue; however, Mankind has the experience of one encounter with Titivillus to make him wiser and, perhaps, better prepared for the next time his faith fails him, and he succumbs to temptation in some form, which will once again put Mankind in the Devil's proximity. After Mankind's departure Mercy points out to the audience that Mankind's fate has been exhibited before them and exhorts them to change their evil habits. Finally, Mercy asks God's mercy on the audience and includes a prediction in his last proposition: Mercy tells the audience that God's mercy will allow them to have eternal life in heaven. The transformation of supposition and the predictive mood appear in this proposition.

An analysis of the linguistic structure of *Mankind* based on Levi-Strauss's theory of binary oppositions, Todorov's ideas concerning equilibrium-disequilibrium-equilibrium as basic plot structure and his theories regarding transformations, propositions, sequences, and moods, and the processes of transformational grammar support the notion that the author of the play was a man of sophistication and education who has creatively used the well-known conflict between Good and Evil as the foundation for a finely constructed drama. The problem of weak faith is as old as the Good-Evil dichotomy, but age does not make it any less a threat to the soul which must contend with the alluring temptations of an increasingly materialistic society brought on by the changing social and economic structure. The playwright must have recognized these dangers to the soul in the medieval world, although such a thing cannot be verified. His play, however, reflects the consequences to the soul which cannot maintain a strong enough faith to control the natural desires of the body and to keep its focus on the spiritual things of life. Such an internal and external conflict between Good and Evil is familiar, but the author of *Mankind* uses this familiar conflict creatively as the binary opposition underlying the structure of the morality play, which appears on the surface as the body-soul image, the horse-rider image, and the Christ's knight image, among others. Other dichotomies in the surface structure are rooted in the Good-Evil binary opposition, such as Truth-Lies, Work-Idleness, Christianity-the Occult, Life-Death, and Positive-Negative. The plot structure of the play moves from the initial state of equilibrium, defined by Mercy as the constant state of temptation, a constant struggle between Good and Evil both within one's own body and in the world at large, to the state of disequilibrium in which Mankind has defected to the side of Evil and back to a state of equilibrium. The new state of equilibrium features a Mankind who is wiser for his experiences and will be better prepared next time he meets Titivillus. The force which creates the disequilibrium is Titivillus's lies. He deceives Mankind into impatiently giving up work and religious faith, which are his only defenses against the Devil. All of Titivillus's lies are believed. Mankind's pride at defeating the Three N's softens the ground and makes it fertile for Titivillus's lies. The force that finally overcomes Mankind's pride is Mercy's truth. Mankind eventually believes Mercy and asks for his forgiveness. The structure of the disequilibrium is a mirror image of the initial equilibrium. In the equilibrium Mankind worships Mercy and Good, but in the disequilibrium he worships Evil, a fact borne out by the similarities in the dialogue of the two sections.

The most important transformation in *Mankind* is that of description, because the characters are usually in a situation of imparting some sort of information to each other. The transformation of attitude is also important and appears often with that of description. The characters make value judgments and then pass those judgments along in dialogue. Abstract verbs such as *warn*, *accuse*, *condemn*, which are popular in the linguistic structure of *Mankind* are often the foundation of the conjoined transformations of description and attitude. The transformations of intention and supposition are valuable in connection with the predictions of characters, such as Mercy and Titivillus, which form a pattern of lateral structural supports in the play. Mercy's predictions concerning Titivillus, his net, and his method of corrupting Mankind come true, as do Mercy's predictions about the Three N's and about finding Mankind. These fulfilled prophecies enhance Mercy's credibility, as well as tie the play together. Those predictions that extend beyond the scope of the play, dealing with accountability and reward in heaven, are more likely to be believed by the audience in light of the predictions that do work out. All of Titivillus's predictions come true, which does not hurt the credibility of the Devil. Medieval audiences tended to take the reality of their perceptions to heart, experiencing right along with the actors. An omniscient Devil is a formidable adversary. Mankind was his, just as Titivillus had predicted, until Mercy's truth saved the day, not to mention Mankind. A strong example of Evil is another creative way the playwright points out the dangers of weak faith and the need to be more spiritual than one truly desires to be.

The transformation of subjectivation achieves prominence during the corruption sequence. Mankind believes Titivillus's lies. The transformation of knowledge is of special import in the return to equilibrium. Mankind finally learns the truth about Titivillus's actions. The transformation of result is most influential in the corruption sequence as Titivillus describes the various stages of the process as accomplished facts. The transformation of appearance is displayed only once in the responses of the Three N's to Titivillus's commands that they give him money, in which they feign poverty. The linguistic structure of *Mankind*, therefore, depends heavily on the transformations of description and attitude with other specific transformations and their corresponding moods appearing more prominently at specific points in the plot development.

The playwright thus skillfully weaves his play around a central binary opposition, Good-Evil, to which all metaphors, images, and dichotomies in the text are connected in some manner. The movement from Good to Evil and back to Good again in the deep structure follows the plot movement from equilibrium to disequilibrium to equilibrium, thereby creating a stronger and a more intriguing structure than a single line plot could ever have produced. The pattern of predictions and fulfillments further enhances the structure along with the images and dichotomies. All of the parts fit nicely together and the familiar struggle between Good and Evil is made unfamiliar enough to qualify as literary art by any standards.

CHAPTER FOUR

Conclusion

In the past the medieval English morality play has not been a favored genre among literary scholars. According to David Bevington, this neglect arises from a judgment that the morality play is fragmented and has no plot or organizing principle; therefore, the morality play has no significance artistically, and one need not spend time studying it (2). Those early critics who bothered to work with the genre found the morality play to be generally lacking in merit of any sort and the authors of such plays to be unsophisticated and "simple minded" (Pollard xliii). *Mankind* is the morality play that seems to have drawn the loudest negative criticism from scholars over the years. Labeled by different scholars at various times as "degraded," "crude," "dirty," *Mankind* has often been referred to as an "ignorant" play directed at a rural audience. The scholars who find anything positive in *Mankind* generally fall into two groups. The first group concentrates on questions about the play, such as the author, the audience, the source, the date, and the time of performance— Christmas or

Shrovetide. The second group, more daring than the first, concentrates on questions arising from the play itself, such as the theme and the parts of the play that seem inappropriate to the play as a whole, including the notion that Titivillus is an improper devil, that Mischief is an extra character with no dramatic purpose, and that the scatological humor is in the play primarily to appeal to rural audiences. Although recent scholarly efforts have begun to focus on the play itself, with Kathleen Ashley emphasizing the language and Michael Kelley struggling to prove *Mankind's* literary artistry, none goes far enough in analyzing the manuscript's language and structure to reveal the brilliance of its composition. Certainly few scholars would consider the possibility that the manuscript of any morality play, especially that of *Mankind*, would qualify as literary art. Analysis of *Mankind*, as a representative morality play, using techniques of classical rhetorical analysis and methods derived from those of modern structuralists Claude Levi-Strauss and Tzvetan Totorov, displays the literary artistry of the playwright from several angles. The standard for this literary artistry is based on the theory of defamiliarization of Victor Shklovsky and on the artistic theory of Roland Barthes. The Christian doctrine that is quite familiar to medieval audiences is, therefore, presented in creative ways to dispel the familiarity and to catch the attention once again; all the parts of *Mankind* fit smoothly together "without noise" and with nothing left over.

Although a major criticism of the morality play in general is its fragmented nature, the lack of a controlling principle, and a major criticism of *Mankind* specifically is the presence of inappropriate or extraneous characters and the use of "dirty" humor in a religious play, a rhetorical analysis nullifies these criticisms by proving that *Mankind* is a tightly constructed play in which all of the characters are necessary and appropriate and the scatological humor is an important aspect of the structure. A careful examination of the language of *Mankind* reveals that the playwright uses numerous rhetorical figures, such as figures of repetition, amplification, emotional appeal, allusion, metaphors, similes, and techniques of argument among others, as well as a few vices of language to support the themes and the structure of his play. Since an analysis focused on the actual language of the manuscript eliminates the distraction of individual artistic interpretations of actors in a live performance, the literary artistry of the play can be more fully appreciated than would be possible in a totally dramatic situation. One can see how the playwright deftly manipulates his rhetorical tools to present creatively the extremely familiar conflict between Good and Evil along with the Christian doctrine related to that conflict in such a way as to grasp the attention of the audience, all the while being careful to incorporate all the elements of the conflict into the structure and the themes of the play. The controlling principle in *Mankind* is the metaphor of the game on which the dramatic action is built. Words constitute the method of proceeding in the game. Mercy's opening and closing speeches, which include words of warning and advice based on Christian doctrine, frame the action of the play in which God, the ultimate Good, is represented on earth by Mercy, and the Devil, the ultimate Evil, is represented on earth by Mischief. These earthly representatives square off in a game to win the soul of Mankind. The two major themes in *Mankind* are sovereignty and rhetoric, which are enhanced by other thematic motifs based on Christian doctrine that interlace the structure of the play. The scatological humor supports the themes from the negative standpoint by graphically displaying the state of the sinful soul and is thus thematically and structurally important, rather than merely a concession to an uneducated audience.

Evidence for the game metaphor as the controlling principle of the surface structure is found in the language, the structure, and the medieval literary tradition of sinister comedy. The words "game," "play," "sport" appear several times in the play. Mischief sets up the game when he tells Mercy that he has come to make Mercy a "game" (1. 69). Titivillus corrupts Mankind in the second scene and mockingly says that he has done his "game" (1. 605). In addition to direct words, there are implicit allusions to the idea of game in the form of pieces of game apparatus, such as a net and a football, Titivillus blinds Mankind to the truth with his net, which brings to mind the ancient children's game of Blind Man's Bluff in which a child is blindfolded and then guided by the artistic indirection of the voices of the other players, who do not wish to be tagged. This situation is similar to the lies Titivillus used to guide Mankind toward the side of Evil. New Gyse's request for a football at the end of the second scene after Mankind's possession by the side of Evil ties into the game metaphor. The request is irrelevant except in a symbolic context, because Mankind represents the football in this game between Good and Evil. Whoever has possession of the ball when Mankind dies and ends the game wins the prize—Mankind's soul.

The structure of the play enhances the game metaphor in that the two opposing sides seem to take turns. Mercy's religious rhetoric and his direct connection to God places him on the side of Good, whereas Mischief's refusal to leave until Mercy tells him to go in the Devil's name, along with his evil lifestyle, places him on the side of Evil in the first scene. The two sides each intend to persuade Mankind to join forces with them; consequently, rhetoric is the means of progressing. Mercy's opening speech is a rhetorical masterpiece. Mischief's rhetoric is good, as the play illustrates; however, Mischief is too smart to go head-to-head with Mercy and chooses instead to use mockery and derision to undermine Mercy's ethos, an important aspect of Mercy's rhetorical position, and to cause Mercy's arguments to seem ridiculous and without merit. Although we cannot know for certain because a manuscript sheet containing the actual dialogue is missing at the begining of the first scene, possibly Mercy's eloquence and authority force Mischief to leave, thereby giving Mercy the first turn with Mankind, whom Mercy tries to persuade to give sovereignty over his life to God. Once Mercy has instructed Mankind in Christian behavior, Mercy leaves, allowing Mischief's cohorts, New Gyse, Nowadays, and Nought a chance at Mankind. The Three N's try to lure Mankind away from work, which represents the side of Good, and into a life of sin, but he drives the villains away with his spade. Fearing that Mercy may have won the game, Mischief and the Three N's decide to cheat by calling on Titivillus, the Devil in this play, to intervene. God is in heaven where he should be, but Titivillus is on earth interfering in the game. Titivillus corrupts Mankind, who changes to the side of Evil. Now it is Mercy's turn again. Mischief is afraid that Mercy will get Mankind back if he finds him. New Gyse suggests getting Mankind to commit suicide by hanging himself. Of course, the Evil side wins if Mankind dies unrepentant, but Mercy appears in time to save Mankind from literal physical death. Trying to overcome Mankind's pride to save him from spiritual death tasks even Mercy's grand eloquence in the final episode of the play; however, Mercy finally succeeds and Mankind accepts God's sovereignty. The fact that Mercy again warns Mankind about Titivillus, his invisibility, his net, his lies, indicates that the game is not over, only the first round. The possibility exists that Mankind will meet Titivillus again, or Mercy would not have bothered with a warning. Mankind's initial experience with temptation will help prepare him for the next round with Titivillus and his pals.

The literary tradition of sinister comedy in which hell is presented to the Devil's victims as an "abominable game" or a "blasphemous parody" (McAlindon 329) and in which the comic scenes enhance the moral message of the serious scenes sets a precedent for the idea of the game metaphor as a controlling structural device. To avoid the potential problems of fear and confusion on the part of an audience whose orientation was to participate on some level in the reality of the drama as they perceived it, medieval writers often presented these works which blended serious religious messages with comedy in the form of a diabolical game or as a parody. Sophisticated and intelligent writers were challenged by this form which is characterized by villains or devils who are witty, sneering, deceitful, and intelligent, as well as powerful and treacherous. These comedies are also permeated by irony and mockery. Audiences in the Middle Ages accepted powerful devils with the ability to test men's faith much more readily if the dramatic context were that of a sinister game than if the context were straight drama. *Mankind* fits the description of these comedies with its mixture of the serious and the comic, and its pervasive mockery and irony. Titivillus is a perfect devil in this context, because he is witty, intelligent, deceitful, powerful, and treacherous. With such a literary tradition as a foundation, the notion that *Mankind* is built on the game metaphor is strengthened.

Mercy must rely on his strong ethos and his skill with language in order to persuade Mankind to become God's obedient servant. Mercy's first speech establishes his ethos as God's mediator on earth and in conjunction with Mercy's last speech forms a frame for the action of the play. This first speech also introduces themes and motifs that are woven throughout the action of the play, emphasizing the author's message and providing structural links for the parts of the play. The first stanza establishes the adversaries in the game with God as the subject of the lines and the implied reference to the Devil in the hissing [s] sound, although the Devil is mentioned specifically in later stanzas as "gostly enmy" and "venymousse serpente." This stanza initiates the sovereignty theme by focusing on the need to be God's obedient servant. The thematic motif of Christ's sacrifice for the sins of humanity is introduced in the second stanza in the form of the "dere bought" oath, which is Mercy's favorite oath and echoes throughout the play, providing structural connections. The simile comparing Christ to a lamb introduces the water imagery that connects to similar imagery in the action of the play when Mankind compares Mercy to a "well" of virtue. Other Christian motifs that start in the frame and pervade the action are the notions of honest work, good deeds, avoidance of idleness and the transitory things in life, and the idea of focusing one's eyes on heaven not on the earth. Mercy's advice is summed up in the corn proverb, which ends his speech. The corn is saved and the chaff is burned. If people give God sovereignty over their lives, they can be the corn that is saved and goes to heaven. This tendency to sum up his advice in a maxim stays with Mercy throughout the play and further enhances his ethos, because people trust others who use proverbs and maxims. The grain proverb is referred to in other parts of the first scene, forming a connection between the frame and the action. The "reap what you sow" maxim is another facet of the corn metaphor used by Mercy later in the play to underscore the notion of accountability for one's deeds that is set up in the initial speech and infiltrates the action. The grain metaphor is also used by the author to support his sovereignty theme from a negative angle by having the minions of the Devil imitate and mock this proverb at various points in the action. The playwright uses the same technique with the "dere bought" oath, which he places in the mouths of Mischief and New Gyse to heighten the irony of the situation, as well as to form structural ties.

Many of the motifs Mercy introduces in the initial speech are picked up in the last speech to close off the framework device. For example, the idea of God's sovereignty over all Mankind as a protection from the venomous serpent (1. 40) is reflected in the reference to Mankind's protection from wicked captivity (1. 905) in the last speech. Christ's sacrifice for humanity's sins, which is ensconced in the "dere bought" oath and reverberates through the action of the play, is tied up at the end in the notion of Christ's love of mankind as the reason that God sent his Son to earth to assume human form (1. 906). Implicit in the assumption of human form is Christ's eventual death for the sins of mankind. Mercy's warning to avoid transitory things (1. 30) in his opening speech connects to his warning in the final speech that the world is a "vanity" (1. 909). Accountability for one's actions, mentioned in the opening speech (1. 42), echoes in Mercy's warning that there will be a "dew examinacion" (1. 908). Finally, Mercy asks God's mercy on the audience in the last lines of the play, which is the same request that he makes in the opening speech (1. 41). These motifs begin in the frame, weave in and out of the action, supporting the themes of sovereignty and rhetoric at various points and providing structural links for the parts of the play, and culminate in various reflections of the same motifs in the framework at the end of the play.

The rhetoric theme, the second major theme in the play, also appears in the framework but indirectly rather than in a direct fashion. In addition to the elevated eloquence of Mercy's vocabulary and the numerous rhetorical devices of the opening speech, the hissing [s] sound, also signals the importance of rhetorical techniques, as well as the presence of the Devil. The first and last stanzas of the opening speech each contain 21 instances of the [s] sound, thus forming a frame around the central stanzas of the speech, just as the speech itself combines with the last speech to form a frame for the entire play. This is rhetorical virtuosity at its best. Within the action of the play, many references to language and its use are found, especially since words are the means of progressing in the game. This theory is supported by Mischief's remark that he "arguyde" with Mercy at the beginning of the "game" (ll. 417–18), by the Three N's request of Titivillus to "speke" to Mankind about his hurting them (l. 496), by Titivillus's remark that he will "speke" to Mankind to lure him from his good habits (l. 528), and by the emphasis on the word "whisper" in the corruption scene, not to mention the emphasis on language and its use throughout the play. Mercy upbraids Mischief for interrupting his "talking delectable" (l. 65) and later compliments the villains on their use of rhetoric: "Few words, few and well sett" (l. 102). New Gyse responds to this compliment with "Many wordys and schortely sett" as constituting the "new gyse" and "þe new jett" (ll. 103–04), which effectively ties the theme of rhetoric into the new fashion. Mercy also discusses idle language often in the play, pointing out to New Gyse and his cohorts that they will be accountable for every word on Judgment Day and indicting those villains for practicing both idle language and idle lifestyles in his judicial oration (ll. 161–85).

In addition to oral language the written word is also emphasized in the mock manor court episode in which Nought records the proceedings. Mischief stresses how the writing looks rather than what it says, another vote for empty rhetoric. Mischief refers to Nought as our "Tulli," which scholars agree is a reference to Cicero, the master rhetorician of Rome. Throughout the play Mercy emphasizes the moral purpose behind language both directly in his own speeches and indirectly in his chastisement of the rogues for their idle language, which often contains scatology and mockery. The importance of moral purpose in language is a hallmark of Quintilian's rhetorical theory, although no mention is made of him in the play. The reference to Cicero indicates an acquaintance with that rhetorician, especially in light of the legal context, and strengthens the idea that the playwright might also have been aware of Quintilian's theory and applied it to Mercy's speeches.

The new jacket that the Three N's make out of Mankind's long robe and give to him in the "initiation" portion of the mock manor court episode symbolizes the new fashion in language, as well as clothing, since New Gyse unites rhetoric and the new fashion in an earlier speech. The jacket symbolizes Mankind's initiation into the ranks of the champion practitioners of empty rhetoric. This jacket may symbolize rhetoric from yet another angle, because this jacket may be a vestige of the influence of *Piers Plowman*, which scholars believe has been noted in other aspects of *Mankind*. Haukyn's jacket stained with sin represents the state of his soul. Mankind's fashionable new short jacket, denoting his new status as a member of the forces of Evil, who thrive on lies and corruption, also represents the state of his soul. Haukyn himself is connected with language abuse and empty rhetoric in that he lies, gossips, and uses his tongue for revenge. In a similar manner Mischief and his cohorts lie about Mercy and mock him derisively. Titivillus uses language to corrupt Mankind, thus gaining revenge for the injuries of the Three N's. The Bible states that language reflects the heart and soul, a fact medieval audiences would know, thereby underscoring the rhetoric theme from another perspective. The empty words of the villains reflect their empty souls.

The liar's contest among the Three N's sets up the collection scene, which is a clever way to tie empty rhetoric into the materialistic values of the transitory world and support both ideas at once. The rhetorical footwork of the three rogues in the face of the Devil, who knows they lie when they say they have no money, is amazing. Each one uses a lie that tops the lie of the last speaker. This display of bold deceit warns the audience in a subtle way to beware of such smooth talkers.

Two examples of the power of words, which emphasize the need for care in language usage, are found in the references to the "neck verse" and in Mankind's badge. The "neck verse" is a Latin Bible verse which a convicted man could recite or read to save himself from hanging. Mankind's badge is a note that he writes and places around his neck to protect him from superstitious charms. Both instances show the power of words to save one from harm and possibly even death.

The playwright skillfully employs his power with words to create major images to emphasize different facets of the sovereignty theme and the supporting motifs. For instance, Mercy uses the horse image to illustrate graphically the point of his speech on moderation and to support the sovereignty theme. The horse that is overfed will not obey his master and will throw him into the mire. If Mankind fails to practice moderation and over-indulges in the sensual pleasures of the materialistic world, then Mankind (the horse) will throw off the sovereignty of God (the master). Since the horse-master metaphor is a common literary symbol for the body-soul dichotomy, a connection already exists between these images. The fleshly desires of the body throw off the spiritual wishes of the soul, which lands in the mud. This image thus unites the scatological humor with the imagery at the heart of the play. The idea of a muddy soul is reflected in the dirty rhymes and scenes in which characters befoul themselves with excrement, vividly displaying the filth of their souls for the world to see. Horse-master and body-soul images thus join together to support the sovereignty theme from two angles at once and to link with the scatological humor, which depicts the consequences of failure to submit to God's sovereignty, thereby achieving support for the sovereignty theme from the negative side as well. The husband-wife image introduces the sovereignty theme from the domestic angle in the action of the play in the segment with Nowadays and his wife

Rachel. The possibility exists that this segment might have been influenced by similar treatment of the same theme, domestic sovereignty, in Chaucer's *The Canterbury Tales*, a possibility that would further enhance the theory of the sophistication and intelligence of the author of *Mankind*. New Gyse links the husband-wife image with the horse-master image when he says that he feeds his wife so well that she is the master, and she abuses him. The initial instance of the body-soul image occurs when Mankind laments the power of his physical yearnings to overwhelm the spiritual desires of his soul. Mercy ties the body-soul image into the horse-master image when he points out that idle living will allow Mischief to put a "bridle" on Mankind. Mankind then connects the body-soul image to the husband-wife image by using a husband-wife metaphor to lament the body's control of the soul (1. 200).

The horse-master image, the body-soul dichotomy, and the husband-wife image all turn on the reversal of the natural order of things, thereby tying these major images into Mercy's judicial oration (11. 162–85), which convicts New Gyse and his friends of being worse than beasts, because they violate the natural order of things. The scatological humor is a pictorial representation of the behavior of beasts, especially when Mischief and Nought befoul themselves. These scenes have a hint of the reversal of the natural order of things in that filth belongs on the ground, not on people. The message is that one must be God's obedient servant or risk violating the natural order of things.

In addition to his clever use of imagery, the playwright supports three principal ideas in the play with a single reference to Job with whom Mercy subtly compares Mankind. Job is connected to rhetoric by his total commitment to the Word of God, which he values above life itself, a fact which emphasizes the power and importance of language. Job also connects to the scatological humor through the fact, reported by Gregory the Great, that Job sat on a dunghill to remind himself of the filth of the flesh. Finally, Job connects to the sovereignty theme by his unquestioning obedience to God in spite of untold adversity. The author, therefore, supports the rhetoric theme, the sovereignty theme, and the scatological humor with one word, a rhetorical feat in itself.

Titivillus offers another example of this technique of gaining support for three major ideas with one reference. Titivillus is linked with rhetoric by literary tradition through the demons of the same name who collected skipped syllables and recorded misdeeds in religious services. Titivillus also is the epitome of the witty, intelligent, ironic and deceitful villain in the tradition of sinister comedy, which revolves around the concept of the diabolical game. Finally, Titivillus is God's adversary in the contest for sovereignty over Mankind's soul. The underlying game metaphor and the two major themes, sovereignty and rhetoric, are thereby rolled into one character.

A rhetorical analysis of *Mankind* reveals the author's considerable ability to use language and imagery creatively to support the themes and the structure of the play. The well-known Christian ideals take on new meaning displayed in metaphors and images that intertwine with each other, exposing different facets of the major themes. All of the parts are essential to the meaning of the play. Mischief is an integral character. Titivillus is exactly the kind of devil needed for the play. The collection scene supports the materialism motif, among other things, and the scatological humor reflects the nature of the villains' souls, as well as serving thematic and structural purposes. Using the theories of Levi-Strauss and Todorov to approach the linguistic structure from another angle exposes a view of this well-constructed play different from the one revealed by the rhetorical analysis. A rhetorical analysis allows one to see the images, themes, and motifs as finished products, whereas an analysis of the ways in which the language of the play functions allows one to see the processes involved in achieving this tightly knit structure. As a result the literary artistry of the author is seen from a new point of view.

In order to gain this perspective on the play, a method of analysis based on Levi-Strauss's major structural principle, the binary opposition, Todorov's theory of plot structure, and his theories concerning propositions, sequences, moods, and transformations has been used in conjunction with some of the basic processes in transformational grammar. Levi-Strauss's theory of binary opposition, which allows the complexities of the reality of a situation to be reduced to the simplest possible pair of opposites, and Todorov's theories of minimal plot structure need no adaptation for an analysis of a morality play. Todorov's definitions of transformations, sequences, and moods, however, have been changed and some new transformations and moods have been added to fit the needs of a dramatic analysis. Since the essence of drama is action, the dialogue of the text has been used to indicate the action occurring between characters in the absence of a dramatic presentation, and the transformations have been applied based on both the action and the dialogue, with no regard for Todorov's distinctions between simple and complex transformations. Both levels of the dramatic construct are therefore necessary in a careful evaluation of the way the language functions in a play. The basis for deciding which transformation or transformations have taken place is the abstract verb in the deep structure, which describes the action that is concretely depicted in the predicates of the propositions. The deep structure in this analysis refers to the abstract area where the seeds of dramatic inspiration first take shape before moving to the surface as action and dialogue. Todorov's transformation of description has been expanded to include the present as well as the past and all information, advice, or knowledge passed on to other characters. Other transformations created on the basis of simple operations in transformational grammar have been added to Todorov's system to cover all situations in a dramatic analysis. The transformations of command, request, and analogy, which covers the operation of metaphors and images from the deep to the surface structure, are additional transformations incorporated into this analysis. The transformation of negation is simply a name change of Todorov's transformation of status in an effort to achieve clarity and avoid confusion. The imperative mood has been added to Todorov's moods, and his indicative mood has been expanded to include both past and present actions along with stated facts. Todorov's definition of sequence has been changed to refer to a specific interaction of characters concerned with a certain topic of conversation or a single situation. The sequence changes when the focus of the situation changes, or when there is a new alignment of characters. Sequences combine to form episodes, which deal with the same idea or motif.

Applying this method of analysis adapted from the theories of Todorov and Levi-Strauss to the important verbal structures of the dramatic plotline of *Mankind* reveals the Good-Evil binary opposition to be the major structural principle in the play from which the primary images and dichotomies emerge. Although the deep structural conflict between Good and Evil manifests itself in Mercy's opening speech when Mercy talks about God and the Devil, the most important surface rendition of this binary opposition is the body-soul image introduced by Mankind in his first speech. This image depicts the internal struggle between the materialistic physical desires and the spiritual wishes of the soul. The inner struggle is reflected in the external struggle between God and the Devil for the soul. Although the body-soul image is not introduced until the third episode of the play, this image reflects the normal condition for all mankind, which is the state of equilibrium, defined by Mercy in lines 225–26 as a constant battle between the soul and the body. This image also represents the important thematic motif of weak faith in that the soul must maintain a strong faith in God in order to maintain the balance between Good and Evil. Weak faith allows the body to succumb to temptation and throw off the restraints of the soul, thereby upsetting the balance between Good and Evil. Such a situation causes a movement toward disequilibrium in which Evil has the upper hand in this play. The necessity of maintaining a balance between Good and Evil underscores the notion of moderation in all things, which is Mercy's message in the initial state of equilibrium and is reflected in the imagery. The horse-master metaphor connects to the binary opposition of Good-Evil through the body-soul image. The master must feed the horse moderately to retain control, just as the body must indulge only moderately in the materialistic pursuits of the world in order to maintain spiritual control by the soul. The Christ's knight image also reflects this theory of moderation in the same way. Strong, unrelenting faith is essential to sensible participation in the pleasures of life. Weak faith leads to overindulgence and causes people to turn their eyes from heaven to earth, endangering their souls. Since knights of old were not always able to maintain their excellent virtues in the face of temptation, the use of this Christ's knight image warns the audience that even the best of men must always be on guard against Evil.

In addition to the imagery, many surface dichotomies have their roots in the Good-Evil binary opposition, such as Truth-Lies, Work-Idleness, Christianity-the Occult, Life-Death, and Positive-Negative. The plot structure moves on the basis of the Truth-Lies dichotomy. The initial state of equilibrium involves Mercy's offering aid to Mankind in the constant struggle he experiences between his body and his soul. Mercy represents Good, because he is God's envoy on earth. As such Mercy also stands for eternal life for Mankind if he chooses God's side in the game, which also requires that one work and do good deeds. When the Three N's try to distract Mankind from his work with the lure of the material world, Mankind drives them away with his spade. Mankind's personal pride surfaces only for a brief moment, but the door is opened to temptation. Mankind's faith weakens. Titivillus steps into the picture and, through the force of his lies, corrupts Mankind. The movement toward disequilibrium begins with Mankind's pride, proceeds in rapid strides with Titivillus's lies, and is completed with Mankind's initiation into the ranks of Evil in the mock court sequence. The movement back toward a new equilibrium begins at once as Mercy searches for Mankind. Mercy must use strong persuasive powers, but his truth is the force that overwhelms Mankind's pride and his desire to participate fully in the material world, instituting a new equilibrium in which Mankind is more experienced than he was originally and will have a better chance against the Devil in the next round. The disequilibrium with its lies and Mankind's worship of Evil in the manor court is a mirror image of the initial state of equilibrium with Mercy's truth and Mankind's worship of Good. The Positive-Negative dichotomy is at work here, as in the other smaller instances of mirror images, such as God and Titivillus both as "lord of lords" who test their followers, Mischief's wish for God to send Mankind the gout as opposed to Mercy's request for God's blessing for Mankind, the Titivillus's exhortation to the Three N's to go out and do harm as opposed to Mercy's exhortation to Mankind to work and keep his holy day. Accordingly, the binary opposition of Good-Evil is the structural principle which moves the dramatic plot in the deep structure from Good to Evil and back again and the primary force in the major images and dichotomies of the surface structure.

Although the important verbal structures in the text of the entire play have been broken down into propositions, sequences, and episodes, which have been analyzed with regard to the transformations and moods involved, only those propositions and sequences important in the discussion of the plot structure have been included in this study. A chart diagraming the sequences, episodes, and plot movement is included in Appendix B for additional information, along with a chart detailing the analysis of Mercy's two framework speeches to illustrate the method. The play falls into fourteen episodes exclusive of Mercy's two framework speeches. The largest episode is the Confrontation between Good and Evil, which is composed of three sequences: Mercy-Mischief Interaction; Mercy-3N's Interaction (dealing with dance); and Mercy-3N's Interaction (dealing with rhetoric). The propositions, which often correspond to one or two lines of the text, are too numerous to include individually. The most important transformation in *Mankind* is that of description, because the nature of drama involves the passage of information of some sort between characters, and the most frequent mood is the indicative. The transformation of attitude, involving value judgments, occurs often in conjunction with the transformation of description and offers insight into the characters, even in a morality play in which abstractions are the main characters. For example, Mankind's harsh judgment of the idleness of the Three N's indicated an overreaction reminiscent of one who might suffer a bit from envy or jealousy. Other overreactions combine to indicate the pride Mankind eventually indulges in to his detriment. Abstract verbs, such as *warn, accuse, condemn* are often the foundation of the two transformations. Predictions and prophecies are important as lateral structural supports in the play from the beginning to the end. Mercy and Titivillus both use the transformation of intention, to depict their own plans, and that of supposition, to relate predictions about future events or the actions of another character. Mercy's predictions about Titivillus and the Three N's come true, which strengthens his position on the predictions that exceed the scope of the play, such as the notion of accountability and the entrance to heaven through acceptance of God's mercy. All of Titivillus's predictions come true, underscoring the terrifying power of the Devil, which surely discourages weak faith in God. Propositions involving the transformations of supposition and intention are usually in the predictive mood. The corruption sequence relies on the transformation of subjectivation, because Titivillus spits forth lies as truth and Mankind believes. Titivillus does not pretend that Mercy is dead; he states this situation as fact, thus the transformation of subjectivation is involved, not that of appearance, as in the sequence in which the Three N's pretend their pockets are empty. The transformation of knowledge is most prominent in the last sequence of the play in which Mankind finally regains his balance between Good and Evil and sees Titivillus for the fraud that he is. The transformation of result, which deals with events as accomplished facts, appears regularly in the corruption scene in which Titivillus reports his progress with Mankind's soul in completed sections. These transformations are usually in the indicative mood. Other transformations and moods appear sporadically but with no distinct pattern. The linguistic structure of *Mankind* thus relies strongly on the transformations of description and attitude with the transformations of intention and supposition forming lateral supports throughout the play, and the transformations of subjectivation and knowledge characterizing, respectively, the corruption scene of the disequilibrium and the repentance of Mankind in the new equilibrium.

Combining the information from the rhetorical analysis and the structural analysis strengthens the evidence in favor of *Mankind* as a work of literary art and its author as an intelligent person of sophistication and talent. *Mankind* is not simply religious propaganda unworthy of note as the early critics would have people believe, nor is the play in the accepted morality play form in which Mankind moves through four stages: innocence, temptation, life-in-sin, and repentance (Ramsay clvi). Mankind is born into a state of sin and cannot be innocent. The state of equilibrium in which Mankind is in a constant position of temptation as a result of the struggle between his body (Evil) and his soul (Good) is more consistent with reality, especially in the Middle Ages, than the state of innocence in the traditional four-part structure. Careful examination of the play from the two different perspectives reveals that *Mankind's* foundation in the deep structure is the binary opposition of Good-Evil which manifests itself in the controlling principle of the game metaphor, detailing a match between the forces of Good (God), represented by Mercy on earth, and the forces of Evil (Devil), represented by Mischief on earth. The object of the game is the soul of Mankind, which is the entity described by A. J. Greimas that passes back and forth on the surface between the states of equilibrium and disequilibrium. Although Mercy's opening and closing speeches are technically part of the two states of equilibrium, these speeches also form a framework around the action of the play, with the Good-Evil opposition appearing in both speeches in the opposition between God and the Devil. The author cleverly uses numerous rhetorical techniques on the surface to support his themes of sovereignty and rhetoric, which are each reflections of the Good-Evil binary pair in that God's sovereignty and the truthful rhetoric of Mercy are good, whereas the sovereignty of Titivillus (the Devil) and the empty rhetoric of Titivillus and his followers are evil. The various aspects of Christian doctrine, such as Christ's sacrifice, represented in the "dere bought" oath, and accountability for one's behavior are introduced in Mercy's opening speech and then weave in and out of the action of the play, providing thematic and structural support. Reinforcing this situation are the predictions and prophecies of Mercy and Titivillus, which utilize the transformations of intention and supposition, and form lateral supports throughout the play, in addition to emphasizing the truth of Mercy's doctrine and the awesome power of the Devil.

The playwright's images are also so tightly intertwined with each other and with the themes they support, as well as with the Good-Evil binary opposition that spawned them in the deep structure, that the play resembles a kaleidoscope, revealing different patterns with each new twist. The body-soul image, the horse-master image, the husband-wife image, and the Christ's knight image are all bound together in some way at various points in the action, as they display different facets of the major themes and motifs. The much maligned scatological humor, which illustrates the contamination of the souls of Mischief and the Three N's, depicts the consequences of failure to submit to God's authority for all the world to see. By reflecting the two major themes and the game metaphor in the character of Titivillus and tying the reference to Job into both themes and the scatological humor, the author displays his rhetorical expertise and his artistic talent. Skillfully employing surface renditions of the Good-Evil binary pair, such as Truth-Lies, Life-Death, and Positive-Negative, the playwright moves his dramatic plot, emphasizes from another angle the consequences of failure to submit to God, and points up the consequences of weak faith, a principle focus of *Mankind*. The Positive-Negative dichotomy finds further support in the rhetorical parallels in the text between sequences, which are mirror images of each other, such as those in the states of equilibrium and disequilibrium with Mankind's worship of Good and then Evil. These mirror images in *Mankind* display Culler's "reversible universe" theory discussed in Chapter One.

The abstract verbs which are prevalent in Mercy's speeches— *warn, teach, accuse, beseech*— combine with the important transformations of description and of attitude to reveal the author's artistry from yet another angle. A priest in a religious service does similar things, directly imparting information and advice, making judgments about behavior, and warning his listeners to change their ways. The deep structural analysis indicates that the glossy rhetoric and lovely linguistic techniques of the surface text present the same messages the audience is very familiar with in such a way that the doctrine seems different enough to catch the attention. The prevalence of the figure commoratio in which the same thing is said in different ways lends additional support to this idea. The imagery and other figures are subtle enough to infiltrate the imagination in any event. The warning about the invisible Evil in a world growing more commercial and materialistic each day that forces all men to be on their guard against a weakening in their faith in God is presented in the characters, the action, the imagery, and in all aspects of the play. All of the parts fit together smoothly. The standard of literary art set by Shklovsky and Barthes has been more than satisfied by *Mankind*. Such virtuosity and talent with language coupled with the indications provided by the possible allusions to or influence by, important authors and rhetoricians, such as Chaucer, Langland, and Cicero, support the theory that the author was an educated, sophisticated man far from being "simple minded." Such a well-constructed play could appeal to an educated audience in the city just as easily as a rural one in the villages.

The use of both a rhetorical and a structural approach to *Mankind* has yielded many insights with regard to its themes, linguistic structure, and the nature of the play itself. The two methods work well together, fostering support from different angles for similar notions and revealing new ideas out of the scope of one or the other of the two approaches. The rhetorical and structural analyses of *Mankind* encourage an objective viewpoint, because the different perspectives provided by the separate requirements of the two methods eliminate any preconceived attitudes and stimulate new thoughts. Such an approach might be useful with other morality plays. The fact that *Mankind*, the morality play that scholars love to heap abuse upon, proves to be a well-constructed example of literary art suggests that other morality plays are probably more than worth the time required to study them. Since the Good-Evil binary opposition is present in all morality plays, Levi-Strauss's theory works quite well in revealing layers of meaning in the play through other dichotomies that emerge. The theory could even be extended further in *Mankind* than this study has undertaken to do. The patterns of transformations in which the transformation of subjectivation characterizes the corruption scene and that of knowledge the new equilibrium and in which the transformations of supposition and intention indicate prophecies and predictions that create lateral supports might be useful in studying other morality plays or, perhaps, in studying the genre itself.

WORKS CITED

Books

Aristotle. *The Rhetoric of Aristotle.* Trans. Lane Cooper. 1932. Englewood Cliffs: Prentice, 1960.

Artz, Frederick B. *The Mind of the Middle Ages: An Historical Survey A.D. 200-1500.* 1953. Chicago: U of Chicago P, 1980.

Barthes, Roland. *A Barthes Reader.* Ed. Susan Sontag. New York: Hill, 1982.

Bennett, H. S. *Chaucer and the Fifteenth Century.* Vol. 2.1 of *The Oxford History of English Literature.* 3 vols. to date. Oxford: Clarendon, 1947.

Bevington, David. *From Mankind to Marlowe: Growth of Structure in the Popular Drama of Tudor England.* Cambridge: Harvard UP, 1962.

Chambers, E. K. *English Literature at the Close of the Middle Ages.* Vol. 2.2 of *The Oxford History of English Literature.* 3 vols. to date. Oxford: Clarendon, 1945.

Coogan, Sister Mary Philippa. "An Interpretation of the Moral Play, *Mankind.*" Diss. Catholic U of America, 1947.

Craig, Hardin. *English Religious Drama of the Middle Ages.* Oxford: Clarendon, 1955.

Culler, Jonathan. *The Pursuit of Signs: Semiotics, Literature, Deconstruction.* Ithaca: Cornell UP, 1981.

—. *Structuralist Poetics: Structuralism. Linguistics, and the Study of Literature.* Ithaca: Cornell UP, 1975.

Davenport, W. A. *Fifteenth-Century English Drama: The Early Moral Plays and Their Literary Relations.* Cambridge: Brewer, 1935.

Eccles, Mark, ed. *The Macro Plays: The Castle of Perseverance, Wisdom, Mankind..* London: Oxford UP, 1969.

Elam, Keir. *The Semistics of Theatre and Drama.* London: Metheun, 1980.

Fifield, Merle. *The Rhetoric of Free Will: The Five- Action Structure of the English Morality Play.* Diss. U Leeds, 1974. Ilkley, Eng.: Scholar, 1974.

Hawkes, Terence. *Structuralism and Semiotics.* Berkeley: U of California P, 1977.

Holman, C. Hugh. *A Handbook to Literature.* 4th ed. Indianapolis: Bobbs, 1980.

Joseph, Sister Miriam. *Rhetoric in Shakespeare's Time: Literary Theory of Renaissance Europe.* 1947. New York: Harbinger, 1962.

Kelley, Michael R. *Flamboyant Drama: A Study of The Castle of Perseverance, Mankind, and Wisdom.* Carbondale: Southern Illinois UP, 1979.

Langland, William. *Piers the Ploughman.* Trans. J. F. Goodridge. Harmondsworth, Eng.: Penguin, 1959.

Lanham, Richard. *A Handlist of Rhetorical Terms: A Guide for Students of English Literature.* Berkeley: U of California P, 1969.

Levi-Strauss, Claude. *The Savage Mind.* Trans. George Weidenfeld. Chicago: U of Chicago P, 1966.

—. *Totemism.* Trans. Rodney Needham. Boston: Beacon, 1963.

MacKenzie, W. Roy. *The English Moralities from the Point of View of Allegory.* New York: Gordian, 1966.

"Menis." *The Middle English Dictionary.* 1970 ed.

Miller, Joseph H., Michael H. Prosser, and Thomas W. Benson. Preface. *Readings in Medieval Rhetoric.* Eds. Joseph H. Miller, Michael H. Prosser, and Thomas W. Benson. Bloomington: Indiana UP, 1973. xi–xvii.

Murphy, James J., ed. *A Synoptic History of Classical Rhetoric.* New York: Random, 1972.

Pollard, Alfred W. Introduction. *English Miracle Plays, Moralities, and Interludes.* Ed. Alfred W. Pollard. Oxford: Oxford UP, 1927.

Potter, Robert. *The English Morality Play: Origins, History, and Influence of a Dramatic Tradition.* London: Routledge, 1975.

Ramsay, Robert Lee. Introduction. *Magnyfycence: A Moral Play.* Bv John Skelton. London: Oxford UP, 1958.

Richards, Lawrence O. *Expository Dictionary of Bible Words.* Grand Rapids: Regency-Zondervan, 1985.

Rossiter, A. P. *English Drama from Early Times to the Elizabethans.* London: Hutchinson, 1950.

Scholes, Robert. *Structuralism in Literature.* New Haven: Yale UP, 1974.

Taylor, Warren. *Tudor Figures of Rhetoric.* Whitewater, WI: Language, 1972.

Todorov, Tzvetan. *The Poetics of Prose.* Trans. Richard Howard. Ithaca: Cornell UP, 1977.

Zesmer, David. *Guide to English Literature from Beowulf through Chaucer and Medieval Drama.* College Outline Series 53. New York: Barnes, 1961.

WORKS CITED

Periodicals

Ashley, Kathleen M. "Titivillus and the Battle of Words in *Mankind*." *Annuale Mediaevale* 16 (1975): 128–50.

Baker, Donald C. "The Date of *Mankind*." *Philological Quarterly* 42 (1963): 90–91.

Brewer, D. S. "Images of Chaucer 1386–1900." *Chaucer and Chaucerians: Critical Studies in Middle English Literature*. Ed. D. S. Brewer. University: U of Alabama P, 1966. 240–70.

Clopper, L. M. "*Mankind* and Its Audience." *Comparative Drama* 8 (1974–75): 347–55.

Conley, John. " 'Reson' in *Mankind*." *Notes and Queries* 23 (1976): 447–48.

Jambeck, Thomas J. and Reuben R. Lee. "Pope Pokett and the Date of *Mankind*." *Medieval Studies* 39 (1977): 511–13.

Jennings, Margaret. "Titivillus: the Literary Career of the Recording Demon." *Studies in Philology* 74 (1977): 1–96.

Keiller, Mable. "Influences of Piers Plowman on the Macro Play of Mankind." *PMLA* 26 (1911): 339–55.

MacKenzie, W. R. "A New Source for *Mankind*." *PMLA* 27 (1912): 98–105.

McAlindon, T. "Comedy and Terror in Middle English Literature: The Diabolical Game." *Modern Language Review* 60 (1965): 323–32.

Neuss, Paula. "Active and Idle Language: Dramatic Images in *Mankind*." *Medieval Drama*. Ed. Neville Denny. Stratford-Upon-Avon Studies 16. New York: Crane, 1973. 41–67.

Pearsall, Derek. "The English Chaucerians." *Chaucer and Chaucerians: Critical Studies in Middle English Literature*. Ed. D. S. Pearsall. University: U of Alabama P, 1966. 20–29.

Pollack, Rhoda-Gale. "Demonic Imagery in the English Mystery Cycles." *Theatre Notebook* 32.2 (1978): 52–62.

Potter, Robert. "Divine and Human Justice." *Aspects of Early English Drama*. Ed. Paula Neuss. Totowa, NJ: Barnes, 1983. 129–34.

Schmitt, Natalie C. "Idea of a Person in Medieval Morality Plays." *Comparative Drama* 12 (1978): 23–34.

Smart, W. K. "*Mankind* and the Mumming Plays. *Modern Language Notes* 32 (1917): 21–35.

—. "Some Notes on *Mankind*." *Modern Philology* 15 (1916): 45–58.

—. "Some Notes on *Mankind*— Concluded." *Modern Philology* 14 (1916): 101–21.

Stock, Lorraine K. "Thematic and Structural Unity in *Mankind.*" *Studies in Philology* 72 (1975): 386–407.

Williams, Arnold. "The English Moral Play before 1500." *Annuale Mediaevale* 4 (1963): 5–22.

APPENDIX A

Todorov's Simple and Complex Transformations

Todorov delineates six types of simple transformations and discusses how each relates to the narrative action. The first simple transformation Todorov describes is the transformation of mode, which concerns "the possibility, impossibility, or necessity" of action and is often expressed in the text by such modal verbs as *ought* and *may* (226). The transformation of intention is next on Todorov's list. This transformation reflects the intention of the subject of the proposition to do something, not the act itself, and is indicated by verbs, such as *intend* and *try*. The transformation of result occupies third place on the list and deals with an action that is an accomplished fact. Verbs useful in expressing this operation are *obtain* and *succeed in* (226). A fourth transformation is that of manner. This transformation designates "the manner in which an action occurs," and, as Todorov explains, could easily describe all the simple transformations; however, he feels this distinction is necessary. Although adverbs usually denote this operation, it can be performed by auxiliary verbs, such as *strive* and *dare* (227). The transformation of aspect deals with the aspects of the verb and is very similar to that of manner. This transformation has its clearest expression, according to Todorov, in auxiliary action words such as *finish* or *begin* (227). The last simple transformation in the group is the transformation of status, which replaces a positive predicate with a negative or contrary predicate (227). The signal for this grammatical operation is the word *not* to express negation or a "lexical substitution" to express opposition (227).

Complex transformations which deal with the action of two predicates rather than one are also divided into six groups by Todorov. The first of these transformations is the transformation of appearance, which reflects an action that appears to be happening, but in reality this action is not happening at all. Verbs that alert one to the presence of this operation are *claim, pretend, feign* (228). Of the two predicates involved, the action of one is not realized, as in this sentence: "Mary pretends that she is sleeping." The transformation of knowledge is the second of the complex transformations. This transformation seeks to gain knowledge concerning the action of the second predicate and is usually denoted by such verbs as *guess, observe, learn*. A transformation that works closely with the transformation of knowledge is that of description. The transformation of description draws a connection between the actions that yield knowledge, relying on such verbs as *to report, to explain, to tell* (228). This operation can be seen in this sentence: "Mary told her mother that Billy broke the lamp." The transformation of supposition deals with actions that have not yet occurred. This transformation differs from the others in that the main predicate is in the future tense, not the present or the past as in the other transformations. Verbs such as *suspect, anticipate, expect, foresee* herald the presence of this grammatical operation (228-29). This transformation deals with prediction and can be seen in this sentence: "Billy suspects that his sister Mary will inform their mother about his behavior." The last two transformations also differ from the previous four in that these transformations deal with the attitude of the proposition's subject rather than with the relationships between speech and the object of speech, and between knowledge and the object of that knowledge (229). The first of these is the transformation of subjectivation which attributes the action of the main proposition to a subject through the means of an observation. The initial proposition does not have to be true, but the person making the observation has to believe that it is true. This transformation is revealed through the verbs *believe, consider, think* (229). The other transformation is the transformation of attitude, which differs from the transformation of manner because the latter concerns the predicate rather than the subject. Todorov defines this operation as the "descriptions of the state provoked in the subject by the main action in the course of its duration" and points out that it deals with a new predicate (229). This transformation can be seen in this sentence: "Billy is upset that Mary should tell on him."

APPENDIX B

Diagrams and Charts

MANKIND – DIAGRAM OF PLOT STRUCTURE
Binary Opposition: Good – Evil
Dramatic Action: Moves from initial equilibrium (Good) to disequilibrium (Evil) to new equilibrium (Good)

EQUILIBRIUM

SEQUENCE   **EPISODE**

Frame: Mercy's opening speech (Mercy – Audience)

Action:

Mercy – Mischief interaction ⎫
Mercy – 3Ns interaction (dance) ⎬ Confrontation between Good and Evil
Mercy – 3Ns interaction (rhetoric) ⎭

Mercy's judicial oration (Mercy–Audience) — Good denounces Evil

Mankind – Audience interaction ⎫ Mankind confronts Good (worships Good)
Mankind – Mercy interaction ⎬
Mankind – 3Ns interaction (attempts to distract Mankind from labor) ⎬ Mankind confronts Evil
Mankind – 3Ns interaction (Mankind hits 3Ns with spade) ⎭

Successful rebuff of temptation produces pride and sets stage for movement to Disequilibrium.

Mischief – 3Ns interaction ⎫ Reaction of Evil Forces to Failure
Collection scene (3Ns – Audience) ⎭

Titivillus – 3Ns interaction ⎫ Devil's Plan to win Mankind
Titivillus – Audience interaction ⎭

Titivillus – Mankind interaction — Devil applies force (Lies) to dislodge Mankind from Mercy creating Disequilibrium

Mankind gives up work/prayer—vows to change his lifestyle.

Moves into Disequilibrium →

MANKIND – DIAGRAM OF PLOT STRUCTURE
Binary Opposition: Good – Evil
Dramatic Action: Moves from initial equilibrium (Good)
to disequilibrium (Evil) to new equilibrium (Good)

DISEQUILIBRIUM

SEQUENCE	EPISODE
Action:	
Mercy – 3Ns interaction	Mankind now worships Evil
Mankind – 3Ns Mischief interaction	Mock manor court
Mercy – Mankind encounter	Mankind avoids Good
Mercy's Lament (Mercy – Audience)	Good is anguished at loss of mankind

Mercy resolves to regain mankind.
Move back to equilibrium begins.

Mischief – 3Ns interaction	Evil plots to keep Mankind through suicide
Mischief – 3Ns Mankind interaction	
Mercy – Mankind interaction	Mercy Applies force (Truth) to dislodge Mankind from Devil and create new Equilibrium

Mankind accepts Mercy's truth. Faith renewed.

Moves into New Equilibrium →

MANKIND – DIAGRAM OF PLOT STRUCTURE
Binary Opposition: Good – Evil
Dramatic Action: Moves from initial equilibrium (Good)
to disequilibrium (Evil) to new equilibrium (Good)

EQUILIBRIUM

SEQUENCE   EPISODE

Action:
Mercy – Mankind interaction continues ⎤ Mankind goes away
    on new level   ⎦ better and prepared to
                                        face future temptation

Frame:
Mercy's closing speech (Mercy – Audience)

MERCY'S OPENING SPEECH

MERCY = I/SPEAKER AUDIENCE = YOU/ADDRESSEE

	Propositions	Transformations	Mood	Abstract Verbs	Type of Message
1.	Mercy tells the audience that God ought be to be glorified. (ll. 1–2)	Description Mode	Optative	Tell (teach)	Action to performed
2.	Mercy tells the audience that God's sent his Son to be crucified for their disobedience. (ll. 3–4)	Description Result	Indicative	Tell	Christian Doctrine
3.	Mercy tells the audience that they should devote their obedient service to God. (l. 5)	Description Mode	Optative	Tell	Christian Doctrine
4.	Mercy tells the audience that God is lord of all things. (l. 6)	Description Aspect	Indicative	Tell	Christian Doctrine
5.	Mercy tells the audience that God created all things. (l. 6)	Description Result	Indicative	Tell	Christian Doctrine
6.	Mercy tells the audience that God sacrificed his Son to redeem sinners. (ll. 7–8)	Description Result	Indicative	Tell	Christian Doctrine

MERCY'S OPENING SPEECH
MERCY = I/SPEAKER   AUDIENCE = YOU/ADDRESSEE

	Propositions	Transformations	Mood	Abstract Verbs	Type of Message
7.	Mercy tells the audience that Jesus died to purge Mankind of sin. (ll. 9–11)	Description Result	Indicative	Tell	Christian Doctrine
8.	Mercy begs the audience (direct address: "O souerence") to rectify their habits. (l. 13)	Request	Optative	Beg	Action to be performed
9.	Mercy advises the audience to venerate Christ, if they wish to participate in his retribution. (ll. 14–16)	Description Mode	Conditional	Advise	Action to be performed
10.	Mercy tells the audience that he is the mediator for their salvation. (l. 17)	Description Aspect	Indicative	Tell	Christian Doctrine
11.	Mercy commands the audience not to go astray during time of temptation, if they want to be acceptable to God. (l. 19)	Command Mode Negation	Conditional	Command	Action to be performed

MERCY'S OPENING SPEECH

MERCY = I/SPEAKER   AUDIENCE = YOU/ADDRESSEE

Propositions	Transformations	Mood	Abstract Verbs	Type of Message
12. Mercy advises the audience (direct address: "souerence") to purify their souls with good works. (ll. 26–27)	Description Mode	Indicative	Advise	Action to be performed
13. Mercy warns the audience that the Devil will try to corrupt them. (ll. 27–28)	Description Supposition	Predicted	Warn	Christian Doctrine
14. Mercy advises the audience (direct address: "O ȝe souerence") not to value transitory things. (l. 30)	Description Mode	Indicative	Advise	Action to be performed
15. Mercy advises the audience to value heavenly things (spiritual things). (ll. 29–31)	Description Mode	Indicative	Advise	Action to be taken
16. Mercy tells the audience that the members glorify the head. (l. 32)	Description Mode	Indicative	Tell Compare	Doctrine/ Image
17. Mercy tells the audience that the Savior is the head and the Saints are the members. (ll. 29–31)	Description Analogy	Indicative	Tell Compare	Doctrine/ Image

MERCY'S OPENING SPEECH

MERCY = I/SPEAKER AUDIENCE = YOU/ADDRESSEE

Propositions	Transformations	Mood	Abstract Verbs	Type of Message
18. Mercy tells the audience that the Savior feeds the Saints from the river of eternal life. (1. 36)	Description Analogy	Indicative	Tell Compare	Doctrine/Image
19. Mercy tells the audience that the river of eternal life dissolves the bonds of Satan. (11. 39–40)	Description Analogy	Indicative	Tell Compare	Doctrine/Image
20. Mercy asks God to preserve the audience from the devil at the Last Judgement. (1. 41)	Request	Optative	Ask	Doctrine/Image
21. Mercy warns the audience that they will be accountable for their lives at the Last Judgement. (1. 42)	Description	Indicative	Warn	Christian Doctrine
22. Mercy tells the audience that the corn will be saved and the chaff will be burned at the Last Judgement. (1. 43)	Description Analogy	Indicative	Tell	Doctrine/Image

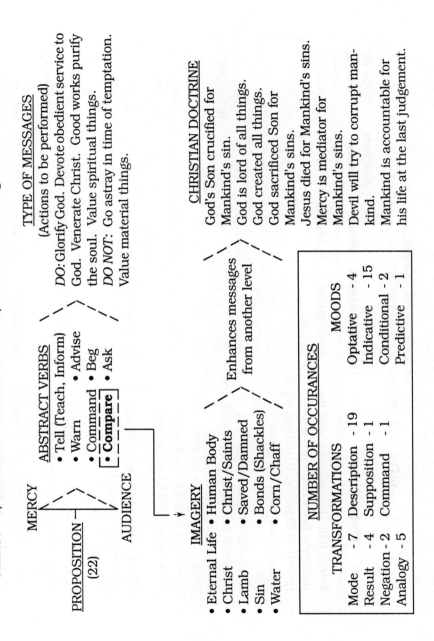

MERCY'S LAST SPEECH

MERCY = I/SPEAKER   AUDIENCE = YOU/ADDRESSEE

	Propositions	Transformations	Mood	Abstract Verbs	Type of Message
1.	Mercy tells the audience that he has done his special property. [parallels Titivillus' departing words that he had done his "game."]	Description Result	Indicative	Tell (inform)	Action Accomplished
2.	Mercy tells the audience that Mankind has been delivered by his benevolent protection.	Description	Indicative	Tell	Action Accomplished
3.	Mercy asks God to preserve Mankind from wicked captivity.	Request	Optative	Ask	Action Desired
4.	Mercy asks God to send Mankind grace to overcome his sensual habits.	Request	Optative	Ask	Action Desired
5.	Mercy commands the audience to examine their own habits.	Command	Imperative	Tell	Action Commanded
6.	Mercy tells the audience to remember that the world is but a vanity.	Description	Optative	Tell	Action Desired

MERCY'S LAST SPEECH

MERCY = I/SPEAKER   AUDIENCE = YOU/ADDRESSEE

	Propositions	Transformations	Mood	Abstract Verbs	Type of Message
7.	Mercy tells the audience that Mankind has proved his wretched conditioned.	Description	Indicative	Tell	Action
8.	Mercy asks God to grant mercy to the audience.	Request	Optative	Ask	Action Desired
9.	Mercy tells the audience that God's mercy will allow them to have eternal life in heaven.	Supposition	Predictive	Foresee	Action to Come